FIVE FINGER EXERCISE

Five Finger Exercise
A Play in Two Acts and Four Scenes

by Peter Shaffer

Harcourt, Brace and Company
New York

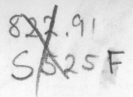
© 1958 by Peter Shaffer

first American edition 1959

Library of Congress Catalog Card Number: 59–10250
Printed in the United States of America

For HARRY and JEAN

PREFACE

BY FREDERICK BRISSON

For one who is a part of the theater and goes to it constantly, there is nothing to equal the thrill of discovery of writing or acting talent. I am fortunate in having an ideal playgoing companion in my wife, Rosalind Russell, whose reaction to stage situations and characters is immediate and acute. She is a keen critic. Her various roles on stage and screen have made her intensely aware of the effort behind creation.

In July 1958, we were in London. We went to a newly opened play that friends told us was the most provocative play staged in England in years. As *Five Finger Exercise* unfolded, a thrill of excitement ran up my spine and I could sense that the same thing was happening to Rosalind and to the audience. Before it was over, I had decided that I wanted to bring this honest and moving first play by Peter Shaffer to America.

Immediately after the show, I phoned Hugh Beaumont, head of the English producing firm of H. M. Tennent Ltd., to tell him how enchanted I had been by the writing, the direction, and the performances. I congratulated him on his gamble on an unknown young author, one who somehow had that rare gift of passing local barriers. The play had perfect identification for my wife and me, two Americans in a British audience. We could understand the gruff father, the culture-loving overpossessive mother, the mixed-up young son, the lonely tutor, the exhuberant young girl; this family could have lived in Larchmont or Brentwood or Palm Beach, or, for that matter, in Neuilly or Gent or Tivoli.

Beaumont was delighted by my conviction that *Five Finger Exercise* should go to America and excited that I felt it was a great woman's play. My partner, Roger L.

Stevens of The Playwrights' Company (we did *The Pleasure of His Company* and *The Gazebo* together last season), had already acquired an interest in the American rights, so Stevens, Beaumont, and I decided to present the play together.

Since the play was new and an enormous success in London, we felt it wise to wait for the 1960–61 season. Also it would have been unthinkable to have entrusted the staging of the delicate fabric of this play to anyone but its original director, John Gielgud.

Five Finger Exercise is intriguingly and aptly named. It concerns five people, and it plays variations on the theme of misunderstood personality, the powerlessness to communicate one's emotional needs to another. It is like a Bach piano piece: seemingly simple, yet interwoven and enormously complicated.

The London critics headlined the emergence of Peter Shaffer with such banner lines as "HIS FIRST PLAY—AND IT'S BRILLIANT" and "NEW WRITER TRIUMPHS WITH FIRST WEST END PLAY." Subsequently, they voted him the most promising new playwright in England. He has made a thunderous impact on the London theater. Peter Shaffer is no "angry young man." He is articulate, meticulously honest, endowed with a fine theatrical awareness. He has a definite future in the theater of the United States as well as in his native land.

I believe that his play will have an effect on American audiences similar to that on British playgoers of dramas by American playwrights. English audiences understood *The Glass Menagerie*, Tennessee Williams' delicate and sensitive study of family life; it didn't matter that it took place in St. Louis, Missouri. They sympathized with Robert Anderson's tormented schoolboy and compassionate housemaster's wife in *Tea and Sympathy*, even though the setting was a New England prep school. They warmed to the young salesman, his wife, and their two children in William Inge's *The Dark at the Top of the Stairs*, though these characters hailed from Kansas, for traveling fathers, bewildered wives, and growing children are universal.

But Peter Shaffer has his individuality. He reveals his personages as starkly to themselves and to the audience as does Ibsen, as elliptically as does Turgenev, but with an air of affectionate, never harsh understanding, and you feel there is a Barrie-like second chance—or hope—for all of them in the future. For some of them life is more than an "exercise"—it is an unfinished symphony.

The Characters

STANLEY HARRINGTON   A furniture manufacturer: in his middle fifties.

LOUISE   His wife: in her middle forties.

CLIVE   His son: nineteen.

PAMELA   His daughter: fourteen

WALTER LANGER   A German boy: twenty-two: employed by Mrs Harrington as tutor to her daughter.

The action of the play takes place in the Harringtons' week-end cottage in Suffolk. The time is the present.

ACT ONE

Scene 1:   A Saturday morning in early September. Breakfast.

Scene 2:   A Saturday night two months later. After dinner.

ACT TWO

Scene 1:   The following (Sunday) morning. Breakfast.

Scene 2:   Sunday night. After dinner.

A multiple set enables us to see a fair amount of this little house: the living-room, the hall, the landing, and the schoolroom where PAMELA *has her lessons.*

The LIVING-ROOM *occupies all of the stage on the ground floor. It is well furnished, and almost aggressively expresses* MRS HARRINGTON'S *personality. We are let know by it that she is a Person of Taste: but also that she does not often let well alone. There is more here of the town, and of the expensive town, than is really acceptable in the country: the furnishings are sufficiently modish and chic to make her husband feel, and look, perpetually out of place. To the left— (all directions are taken from the viewpoint of the audience)— there is a sofa or banquette, and a coffee table. A comfortable armchair bridges the gap between the social centre of the room, and its eating centre. This last is to the right, and slightly more upstage: it is occupied, of course, by a dining table, and chairs to match. The right wall contains the french window, down right, through which comes all the light the room receives— autumn light from an old garden. A door at the back leads into the kitchen. Up centre, against the back wall, stands a sideboard bearing bottles, glasses, a vase of flowers, etc. In the left wall which comes down at right angles to the audience before changing direction to form a scrim behind the sofa, is the door into——*

The HALL. *This can be seen (when lit) through the scrim wall behind the sofa. It is quite small and contains the usual paraphernalia of cottage halls: hats and coats on pegs; Pamela's riding-cap and crop; a sporting print, and perhaps a barometer. The front door opens into it, left, and the staircase of the cottage leads out of it, right, on to——*

The LANDING. *This occupies a fairly small but important central area above the living-room.* WALTER'S *bedroom door opens on to it, right: the door must be recessed and not too prominent; for most of the evening it can even be screened by a curtain. On the left of this, a corridor leads off to two bedrooms (*CLIVE'S *and his parents') and the bathroom—all of which are invisible. On the extreme left a further short flight of steps leads up to——*

The SCHOOLROOM, *which is directly above the sofa area of the living-room. This is very much* PAMELA'S *room: it is littered with her possessions, her books and old toys and clothes. In the centre is a round table where her studies are done, and two chairs. Its right wall contains the door to her bedroom. Its left wall has the window, gaily framed in frilly curtains, a hanging lamp, and a gas fire. The room is brightly coloured, and reflects the liveliness of its chief occupant.*

The whole stage shows a compact dwelling, disposed with feminine care.

ACT ONE

SCENE ONE

A bright Saturday morning in early September.
   CLIVE *is sitting at the breakfast table. He is a boy of nine-teen, quick, nervous, taut and likeable: there is something about him oddly and disturbingly young for his age, the nakedness of someone in whom intellectual development has out-stripped the emotional.* LOUISE, *his mother, comes in with a plate of eggs and bacon for him. She is a smart woman in her forties dressed stylishly, even ostentatiously, for a country week-end. Her whole manner bespeaks a constant preoccupation with style, though without apparent insincerity or affectation. She is very good looking, with attractive features, which are reflected—though with greater insta-bility—in her son.*

LOUISE. (*Looking out of the french window.*) Your father's going back to nature.

CLIVE. How far?

LOUISE. Wait till you see. He's got one of his open air fits. This morning we're going shooting with that dreary stockbroker from the Gables—whatsisname.

CLIVE. Benton.

LOUISE. Yes. Well, to honour Mr Benton he's gone and got himself one of those vulgar American hunting jackets made out of a car rug. Can you imagine anything more ridiculous?

CLIVE. (*Eating.*) He probably saw it in one of those American mags that Chuck left here last week-end. . . . Apart from the jacket, how is he?

11

LOUISE. He's all right. Came down on the six-thirty. What time did *you* get in?

CLIVE. Midnight.

LOUISE. Of course he wanted to know where you were.

CLIVE. And did you tell him?

LOUISE. I didn't know. I supposed you were still in London.

CLIVE. (*Resentfully.*) I was out. O-U-T.

LOUISE. Yes, dear.

CLIVE. Just plain out.

LOUISE. All right, dear. (*She makes for the kitchen.*) Could you manage another egg if I did one quickly? The pan's still hot.

CLIVE. No thanks.

LOUISE *goes out.* STANLEY *comes in from the garden. He is dressed in a brightly-coloured hunting jacket. He is a forceful man in middle age, well built and self-possessed, though there is something deeply insecure about his assertiveness.* CLIVE'S *nervousness instinctively increases with his appearance.*

CLIVE. Good morning.

STANLEY. Morning. (*He takes his place at the table.*)

CLIVE. Very becoming.

STANLEY. (*Vaguely.*) What?

CLIVE. I said 'Very becoming'.

STANLEY. (*Pleased.*) Oh . . . (LOUISE *returns with the toast.*) Where's Pam?

LOUISE. Walter's taken her for a walk before they start their lessons. They've had their breakfast; I'll get you yours. (*To* CLIVE.) Are you sure you don't want anything more, dear?

CLIVE. Quite sure, thank you.

LOUISE. (*Fondly.*) Well, you're having a very good breakfast for a change. I shan't press you.

LOUISE *goes out.*

CLIVE. (*Nervously.*) I think Pam likes to get the French over with early. Still, it's a bit desperate, starting the day with irregular verbs.

STANLEY. (*Brusquely.*) You know who we are? We're millionaires.

CLIVE. What?

STANLEY. Now we've got a tutor we must be. We don't send our girl to anything so common as a school. You like the idea, I suppose?

CLIVE. (*Eager to agree.*) As a matter of fact, I think it's ridiculous. I mean, well, unnecessary.

STANLEY. Your mother thinks different. Apparently the best people have tutors, and since we're going to be the best people whether we like it or not, we must have a tutor too. Herr Walter Langer, if you please. Ten quid a week and a whole term's fees to the school we didn't send her to. Did you know that?

CLIVE. No.

LOUISE *comes in with the porridge for her husband.*

STANLEY. Oh yes. Still, I can afford it. What's money after all? We had a town place so we simply had to have a country place, with a fancy decorator to do it up for us. And now we've got a country place we've simply got to have a tutor.

LOUISE. Are you starting on that again? Well, please remember it's Walter's first week-end down here, and I want everyone to be nice to him. So just keep your ideas to yourself, would you mind? We don't want to hear them.

STANLEY. We? Clive agrees with me.

LOUISE. Oh? Do you, Clive?

CLIVE. (*Quietly.*) Isn't it a little early for this sort of conversation?

STANLEY. You just said you thought a tutor was ridiculous.

CLIVE. Well, not that exactly . . . I mean . . .

He lowers his eyes and proceeds to examine his breakfast with interest.

LOUISE. Get on with your breakfast, dear.

She sits down at the other end of the table and pours the coffee.
STANLEY *regards his son balefully. A slight pause.*

STANLEY. You were in late last night.

CLIVE. (*Avoiding his eye.*) Yes. I—I got involved.

STANLEY. Involved?

CLIVE. Well, I had some work to do in London.

STANLEY. Work?

CLIVE. Well, not exactly work—sort of criticism really. I promised to review something. It's going to be printed.

STANLEY. In a paper?

CLIVE. Sort of paper.

STANLEY. (*Sarcastic.*) Oh, *The Times*, I suppose?

CLIVE. (*Unhappily.*) Well, it's more of a magazine, actually. It's not very—well, famous.

STANLEY. What's it called?

CLIVE. New Endeavour.

STANLEY. New what?

CLIVE. (*Low.*) Endeavour.

STANLEY. Hm. . . . Well, why did they ask you?

CLIVE. It was more me did the asking. You see, the usual man's ill, so I asked this friend of mine—who's a friend of the Editor's—if I could do it, and he said yes. So I did. Anyway, it was two free seats.

STANLEY. What for?

CLIVE. A play.

STANLEY. (*Aloofly.*) Was it any good?

CLIVE. Yes . . . It was splendid, as a matter of fact.

LOUISE. What was it, dear?

CLIVE. Elektra.

STANLEY. What's that?

LOUISE. (*With exaggerated surprise.*) You can't mean it!

STANLEY. Mean what?

LOUISE. You just can't mean it. Really Stanley, there are times when I have to remind myself about you—actually remind myself.

STANLEY. (*Quietly.*) Suppose you tell me, then. Educate me.

LOUISE. (*Loftily.*) Clive dear, tell your father, will you?

CLIVE *sits eating.*

STANLEY. (*To him.*) Well, go on.

CLIVE. (*Low.*) It's Greek.

STANLEY. Oh, one of those.

LOUISE. (*Brightly, putting her husband in his place.*) Who was in it, dear? Laurence Olivier? I always think he's best for the Greek things, don't you? . . . I'll never forget that wonderful night when they put out his eyes—you know the one; you and I went when your father was in Leeds that time. I could hear that scream for weeks and weeks afterwards, everywhere I went. There was something so *farouche* about it. You know the word, dear: *farouche*? Like animals in the jungle.

STANLEY. (*To* CLIVE.) And that's meant to be cultured?

CLIVE. What?

STANLEY. People having their eyes put out.

CLIVE. I don't know what 'cultured' means. I always thought it had something to do with those pearls they sell in Oxford Street.

LOUISE. Nonsense, you know very well what your father means. It's not people's eyes, Stanley: it's the *poetry*. Of course I don't expect *you* to understand.

STANLEY. (*To* CLIVE.) And this is what you want to study at Cambridge when you get up there next month?

CLIVE. Well, more or less.

STANLEY. May I ask why?

CLIVE. Well, because . . . well, poetry's its own reward, actually. Like virtue. All Art is, I should think.

STANLEY. And this is the most useful thing you can find to do with your time?

CLIVE. It's not a question of useful.

STANLEY. Isn't it?

CLIVE. Not really.

STANLEY. (*Staring at him gravely.*) You don't seem to realize the world you're living in, my boy. When you finish at this university which your mother insists you're to go to, you'll have to earn your living. I won't always be here to pay for everything, you know.

CLIVE. (*With a spurt of anger.*) Look, I'm not exactly five years old.

STANLEY. (*Extinguishing it.*) Then it's time you acted your age. All this culture stuff's very fine for those who can afford it; for the nobs and snobs we're always hearing about from that end of the table—(*indicating* LOUISE)—but it's not going to earn you the price of a sausage outside this front door. I mayn't be much in the way of education, but I know this: if you can't stand on your own two feet you don't amount to anything. And not one of that pansy set of spongers you're going round with will ever help you do that. And you know why? Because they've got no principles. No principles worth a damn.

CLIVE. You know nothing about my friends.

STANLEY. *I know.* I've seen them. Arty-tarty boys. They

think it's clever going round Chelsea and places like
that giggling and drinking and talking dirty, wearing
Bohemian clothes. Tight trousers. Who gave them the
right to look down on other people, that's what I want
to know, just because they don't know about the—
(*affected voice*)—*operah* and the *ballay* and the *dramah*?

LOUISE. And who gave you the right to talk about
Bohemian clothes? What are you supposed to be, a
lumberjack?

STANLEY. (*Ignoring her.*) Who did you go with last night?
Well? Who's this friend of the editor?

CLIVE. (*Subdued.*) Chuck.

STANLEY. Oh yes. Your American pal. The one who
stayed here last week-end—sings in cafés and wants to
stay in school till he's thirty, living on grants. Such a
dignified way to go on.

LOUISE. (*Sharply.*) I should have thought it was a sign of
maturity to want to become more educated. Unfortu-
nately, my dear, we weren't all born orphans; we didn't
all go to grammar schools, or work up a furniture factory
on our own by sheer willpower. We can never hope to
live down these shortcomings, of course, but don't you
think you might learn to tolerate them? We just didn't
have the advantage of your healthy upbringing in the
tough world outside.

The effect of this speech is momentarily to crush STANLEY *into
silence.*

Jou-jou, come and help me clear away, dear. I'm going
to get Walter to give me a music lesson later on.

STANLEY. (*Disbelieving.*) Music lesson?

LOUISE. Yes. And don't get yourself shot by mistake.
Though there can't be many birds that colour.

STANLEY. What time's lunch?

LOUISE. Oh, oneish. It depends. After my lesson I'm going to take Walter down to the Bay. I'm going to show him some plants I've found. Did you know he was a botanist as well? And such charm! Well, of course, it's exactly what I've said all along. It takes a Continental to show us just how ignorant we really are. Jou-jou, la porte!

CLIVE *opens the kitchen door for her and she goes through it with a loaded tray.*

STANLEY. (*To* CLIVE.) I'll see you later. That is, unless you want to come shooting with me. No, of course you wouldn't. Well, just see you get out into the air. I didn't take this cottage so you could lounge about indoors all day. You know, Clive, I just don't understand you at all. Not at all.

He goes out into the hall and through the front door, banging it behind him. LOUISE *returns.*

CLIVE. (*With dull rage.*) Breakfast as usual.

LOUISE. (*Clearing.*) Never mind. It was just one of his moods.

CLIVE. Yes. . . .

LOUISE. Oh, Jou-Jou, I want you to be very happy down here, darling. Really happy, not just pretending. After all, it's why I made Daddy buy this place—to get away from the house and London and all the squabbling. To come into the country and relax in our own little retreat. . . . So you've just got to be happy. You can't let me down. Can you?

CLIVE. Votre Majesté. My Empress!

LOUISE. (*Permitting her hand to be kissed.*) Levez!

CLIVE. The Empress Louise, ill fated, tragic, dark-eyed Queen from beyond the seas! What is your wish, Madame? I am yours to command.

LOUISE. I've told you already, my little Cossack. Sois content. Be happy.

CLIVE. Bien. On my honour as a guardsman, and on my beautiful hat of genuine black sheepskin, I promise to you six big laughs a day, and twelve little giggles.

LOUISE. Darling. My darling Jou-jou!

CLIVE. Maman!

They embrace very fondly.

LOUISE. Now that's a promise, you know. To be happy. Then I can be happy too. Because I can tell when you're not, you know: and that makes me miserable also. So remember: no complexes.

CLIVE. No complexes, Majesté.

He bows again. She kisses his forehead.

LOUISE. Come on. I'll wash and you dry. They won't take five minutes.

CLIVE. It'll take at least twenty. I can't think why you don't get a maid in.

LOUISE. Oh Jou-jou, not that again! For one thing, it's three miles to the village and no bus service, so who do you think we're going to get out here? (*Warmly.*) And anyway, my dear, this is meant to be a *retreat*. For just us. Housework's all in the fun. Everyone does it these days. . . .

She gives him a warm smile and leads him into the kitchen. As the scene ends, PAMELA *comes noisily through the front door and races upstairs into the schoolroom. She is followed closely by her tutor* WALTER LANGER, *carrying a bunch of wild flowers.*

PAMELA. (*As she runs.*) If I'm there first, no French today!

WALTER. Oh no, you do not get out of it that way! . . . (*Arriving in the schoolroom.*) Come on. We're ten minutes late already. Now we do the French. (*He puts down the flowers.*)

PAMELA. Oh, it's too cold to think in French, Walter.

WALTER. (*Not to be put off.*) Very well. I light the fire.

He does so. PAMELA *sits resignedly at the table. She is a happy girl of fourteen, as volatile as her brother, but wholly without his melancholy—or the seriousness that touches* WALTER. *The tutor is now seen to be a German youth of twenty-two, secret, warm, precise yet not priggish, and happily at ease with his young pupil.*

Parler. To talk. Future tense. Think hard.

PAMELA. Je parlerai . . . ?

WALTER. Good.

PAMELA. Je parlerai, tu parleras, il parlera, nous—nous parlerons?

WALTER *nods, putting on the spectacles he wears for reading.* Vous parlerez, ils parleront.

WALTER. Good, that's the first time you have it right!

PAMELA. Oh, phooey to French. I hate it. Really.

WALTER. Why?

PAMELA. Because the French are a decadent nation. Personally I think we all ought to study Russian and American.

WALTER. But American is the same as English.

PAMELA. Of course it's not. When they say 'dame' they mean young girl, and when we say 'dame' we mean old girl. But when we call someone 'old girl' we really mean what they call a dame. So you see.

WALTER. No.

PAMELA. Well, of course. I know all about Americans from Mary. You've still to meet her. She's my only friend here.

WALTER. Where does she live?

PAMELA. Over the stables in Craven Lane. You'll just fall when you see her.

WALTER. How? In love?

PAMELA. Of course. Mummy says she's common, but that's just because she wears shocking pink socks and says 'Drop dead' all the time. I know her mother drinks and has lovers and things. But, her husband's dead so you really can't blame her, can you? Just like Clive says: There-but-for-the-Grace-of-God Department.

WALTER. And she knows all about America because she says 'drop dead'?

PAMELA. (*Loftily.*) Of course not. How can you be so brutish? For one thing, she's got an American boy friend in the Air Force.

WALTER. How old is she?

PAMELA. (*Airily.*) Sixteen. But that's all right; they like them young. I don't think they actually . . . well, you know. . . . Sometimes she gets decked up in her black jeans and goes off to some sexy club in Ipswich under a Polish restaurant. But her mother doesn't like her going round the streets looking like that, so she has to sneak off when no one's looking.

WALTER. Like witches.

PAMELA. Witches?

WALTER. Going to their Sabbath.

PAMELA. What's that?

WALTER. When they used to worship the Devil. They used to dress up and sneak off just like that. It was the same thing like the Teddy Boys. You make yourself very excited, then people give you a bad name and start being afraid of you. That's when you really do start worshipping the Devil.

PAMELA. Oh, phooey.

WALTER. (*More gravely.*) Not phooey.

PAMELA. You talk as if you'd seen him.

WALTER. The Devil? I have.

PAMELA. Where?

WALTER. Where he lives.

PAMELA. Where's that?

WALTER. Where I was born.

PAMELA. And what was he doing?

WALTER. Sitting down.

PAMELA. Where?

WALTER. Behind people's eyes . . . (*Seeing her confusion.*) Well, isn't that a good place to sit?

PAMELA. Do you miss it?

WALTER. What?

PAMELA. Your home.

WALTER. It's not my home.

PAMELA. Still, there must be things you miss. Birthdays or Christmases or something.

WALTER. Christmas, yes. In our little town it was better. It's called Muhlbach. The stars are more clear there.

PAMELA. Just the stars?

WALTER. (*With a small spurt of excitement.*) No, ice too. Ice grows all down the river, and at night you go skating all alone, all alone for miles in the black, and it's terribly cold and fast—and suddenly you see torches coming towards you, and voices come, and there's a crowd of happy people with nuts and fruit and hot rum, kissing you a good New Year.

PAMELA. Oh, wonderful!

WALTER. (*With reservation.*) Yes, for that . . .

PAMELA. Let's go! Just for Christmas, you and me. You can teach me enough German in twelve weeks so I can

understand everyone——Oh, I'm sorry. I forgot. You
don't teach German.

WALTER. No.

PAMELA. Walter, I never asked before—but why not? I
mean you'd make more money doing that than anything
else.

WALTER *shakes his head slowly 'No'.*

You're really a very strange young man.

WALTER. Am I?

PAMELA. (*Kindly.*) I suppose part of it's living in a
foreign country all the time.

WALTER. It's not foreign. Not for always, anyway. I've
been here five years, and soon now I get my citizenship.

PAMELA. Then you'll be English?

WALTER *nods 'Yes'.*

Then you'll like Christmas here too, because this'll be
home and you'll spend it with us here in the country.
Don't you have any family at all? (WALTER *shakes his
head.*) No one?

WALTER. No.

PAMELA. But that's the wrong answer. When I say 'Have
you got no family?' you must say: 'Yes, of course I have
a family, and a very fine one too.' Now repeat after me:
'My family lives at 22, Elton Square, London and "The
Retreat", Lower Orford, Suffolk.'

WALTER. My family lives at 22, Elton Square, London
and 'The Retreat', Lower Orford, Suffolk.

PAMELA. Good. Ten out of ten. Now you look much
happier. . . . You should wear a high collar. And one of
those floppy ties. Then you'd look like Metternich or
someone. And wear your hair very sleek and romantic.

She smooths his hair.

Like this. . . .

WALTER. (*Dodging.*) Hey!

PAMELA. No, it's terribly becoming . . . Count Walter
  Langer, Knight of the Holy Golden Soupladle!

She ruffles his hair.

WALTER. Pamela, no!

*He ducks away from the table. She chases him. He grabs the
  flowers and runs down the stairs on to the landing.*

WALTER. Stop it! You're not to——

PAMELA. Pompous, pompous, pompous!

WALTER. Now you stop it or I'll be very cross.

PAMELA. Augustus Pompous!

WALTER. And very sick!

PAMELA. Phooey!

WALTER. I will. You don't believe me . . . ?

LOUISE. (*Calling 'off' from kitchen.*) Walter!

WALTER. (*Standing up.*) There's your mother. I go now.
  What's that in French—'I go'?

PAMELA. Je allez?

WALTER. No, I've told you one million times. Je vais.
  Now you go back and do some history.

PAMELA. Oh, all right. (*She goes back to the schoolroom.*)
  Hey!

WALTER. Yes?

PAMELA. See you anon, Mastodon.

WALTER. Quarter to four, Dinosaur!

He goes downstairs to the living-room. PAMELA *applies herself to the history book, sitting at the table and making notes.
  (Entering the living-room.)* Good morning.

CLIVE. Hullo.

WALTER. Mrs. Harrington was calling me.

CLIVE. She's in the music room through there.

WALTER. You have a music room in the cottage?

CLIVE. Only an outside one. When we took this place it

used to be the scullery, but Mother wasn't daunted by that. She picked up an upright for two pound ten and knocked down a wall to get it in. It's lucky it's at the back because His Godship doesn't care for music.

WALTER. Oh, I'm afraid I was playing my gramophone last night—I'm sorry.

CLIVE. (*Wryly.*) He'll soon tell you if he minds. . . . Tell me, how d'you like being tutor to our little hepcat?

WALTER. Oh, she's delightful. When your mother first met me and invited me to live with you, I—I didn't know what I should find. My last job was . . . not so easy.

CLIVE. You lived with a family too?

WALTER. No. I had a flat in Paddington. More of a basement, really.

CLIVE. I can imagine.

WALTER. This is . . . my first family.

CLIVE. Yes?

WALTER. Yes.

CLIVE. (*Lightly.*) Well, let me give you a warning. This isn't a family. It's a tribe of wild cannibals. Between us we eat everyone we can.

WALTER *smiles.*

You think I'm joking?

WALTER. I think you are very lucky to have a family.

CLIVE. And I think you're lucky to be without one.

He sees a faint distress in WALTER.

I'm sorry. I'm making tasteless jokes. Actually, we're very choosy in our victims. We only eat other members of the family.

WALTER. (*Catching the mood.*) Then I must watch out. Your sister thinks I'm almost a member already.

CLIVE. Pam? You know, I don't like the way she's growing up at all. She wants to *include* people all the time:

she doesn't appear to want to exclude or demolish anybody.

WALTER. Perhaps that's because she takes after her mother.... (*Confused.*) Excuse me.

CLIVE. That's quite all right. A girl who took after Stanley would be almost unthinkable.

LOUISE *comes in from the kitchen, with an album of music.*

LOUISE. Walter, my dear, I do hope I didn't disturb your lesson. I'm simply longing to hear you try my little piano.

WALTER. Mrs Harrington—I play so badly.

LOUISE. Nonsense! You have such beautiful hands. (*She takes one of his hands.*) I remember once shaking hands with Paderewski. Of course it was many years ago, and I was only a girl, but I've never forgotten it. He had hands almost exactly like yours, my dear boy. Much older of course—but the same bone formation, the same delicacy.... This was my Mother's album.

WALTER. (*Putting on his spectacles to examine it.*) It's charming.

LOUISE. What are you going to play for me? Something Viennese, of course.

WALTER. What would you like? Beethoven?—Brahms?

LOUISE. Wonderful! And you can explain to me all about it. I mean where it was written and who for. I always think it so much increases one's enjoyment if you know about things like that. Take the 'Moonlight', for example. Now what was the true story about that?

CLIVE. Well, it wasn't really moonlight at all, Mother. Moonlight was the name of the brothel where Beethoven actually was when he started writing it.

LOUISE. Jou-jou!

CLIVE. He got one of the girls to crouch on all fours so

he could use her back for a table. It's in one of the biographies, I forget which.

LOUISE. (*To* WALTER.) He's being very naughty, isn't he? Really, Jou-jou!

WALTER. (*Picking up the flowers and presenting them to her.*) Mrs Harrington, I found these in the lane. They are quite rare, you know. I thought you might be interested.

LOUISE. (*Very pleased.*) Oh, thank you, Walter. I'm most touched. Aren't they beautiful, Jou-jou? (CLIVE *shrugs.*) You know, I must give you a name. Walter is much too formal. Wait. Of course! (*Taking the idea from his spectacles.*) Clive's Jou-jou, so you can be Hibou. Perfect. Hibou, the owl. (*To* CLIVE.) He looks rather like an owl, doesn't he?

CLIVE. Why not Pou? That's better still——Louse.

LOUISE. Oh, he's impossible this morning. Your father's right: a walk in the fresh air would do you a lot of good.

PAMELA *snaps her book shut and comes bounding out of the schoolroom and down the stairs.*

PAMELA. (*Running downstairs.*) Mother! Mother!

LOUISE. Good heavens, what a noise that girl makes! (*To* WALTER.) I'm afraid you're going to have to teach her some etiquette as well.

PAMELA *comes bursting into the living-room.*

PAMELA. Mother!

LOUISE. Quietly, dear. Quietly.

PAMELA. (*Breathless.*) Sorry. Mother, will you test me on my history?

LOUISE. Ask Clive, will you, dear? I'm busy now. Walter's going to play for me.

PAMELA. Are you, Walter? How nice . . .

LOUISE. (*To* WALTER.) Come along, my dear. We haven't got too much time.

LOUISE *goes out with* WALTER *into the kitchen.* PAMELA *studies her brother, then knocks on the door.*

PAMELA. (*In a coy, exaggerated voice.*) General . . . General Harrington.

CLIVE. (*Old soldier's voice.*) Eh? What's that?

The following dialogue is conducted in these voices.

PAMELA. May I come in?

CLIVE. Well, if it's not little Daphne! Spike me cannon! How very kind of you to call. Come in, me dear. Don't be afraid.

PAMELA. Thank you. (*She minces into the room.*)

CLIVE. And how are you, eh? Eh?

PAMELA. Fine, thank you. And how's the—(*whispers*)—you know-what?

CLIVE. (*Normal voice.*) Do I?

PAMELA. (*Normal voice.*) Gout.

CLIVE. Ah. (*General's voice.*) Oh, it comes and goes, y'know. Comes and goes.

PAMELA. (*Daphne's voice again, gushing.*) I think it's wonderful of you to take it so well. I'm sure I'd be complaining all the time. I'm a real silly-billy about pain.

CLIVE. Nonsense, me dear. Lord, though, how yer remind me of yer dear mother. Hair just like hers. Yellow as a cornflower, I always used to say.

PAMELA. (*Normal voice.*) There's something wrong about that.

CLIVE. (*Normal voice.*) Is there? What?

PAMELA. Cornflowers are blue.

CLIVE. Well, your mother certainly didn't have blue hair.

PAMELA. (*Archly.*) That's all you know. . . . Anyway, you've got to test my history.

CLIVE. (*Beckoning.*) Your ribbon.

Automatically she goes to him for it to be tied. He sits on the couch; she kneels beside him. The sound of piano music from the music room.

PAMELA. (*Listening.*) He's the best, isn't he?

CLIVE. Just about.

PAMELA. Oh, you can tell. I knew just as soon as he came in the door.

They listen for a moment.

CLIVE. How d'you get on together?

PAMELA. Oh, we simply adore each other.

CLIVE. Is he going to teach you anything?

PAMELA. Everything, my dear. Just wait and see, I'll be the most erudine girl for my age in London.

CLIVE. Dite.

PAMELA. What?

CLIVE. Eru*dite*. Well, supposing we make a start.

PAMELA *hands over her list.* CLIVE *studies it earnestly for a moment.*

Which was the most uncertain dynasty in Europe?

PAMELA. I haven't the faintest.

CLIVE. (*As if reading.*) The Perhapsburgs.

PAMELA. Who?

CLIVE. The Perhapsburgs.

PAMELA. Now, Clive, really——

CLIVE. (*Enthusiastically.*) I don't know much about them yet, but I'm working on it. I'll have them fixed by the end of the week. So far there's just Thomas the Tentative—a successor of Doubting Thomas, of course—and Vladimir—the Vague.

PAMELA. That's marvellous! How about a woman?

CLIVE. By all means.

PAMELA. Dorothea.

CLIVE. Nice.

PAMELA. Dorothea the—the Downright.

CLIVE. But that's just the opposite. There's nothing Perhaps about her.

PAMELA. Well, she could be the black sheep of the family.

CLIVE. We'll see. . . . Now. (*He consults the list.*) Pay attention. Who was known as the Crying Cavalier?

PAMELA. (*Protesting.*) No, Clive, seriously—I've really got to——

CLIVE. Answer me. Who?

PAMELA. I don't know.

CLIVE. Who was the Unknown Civilian?

PAMELA. I don't know.

CLIVE. Who was the Curable Romantic?

PAMELA. I don't know. I don't know . . . !

She throws herself at CLIVE. *The music stops.*

CLIVE. Really, you are the most impossibly ignorant child. . . . (*Struggling with her happily.*) Hepcat! Hepcat!

PAMELA. (*Springing away from* CLIVE.) Tell me a story!

CLIVE. Sweet or sour?

PAMELA. Sour.

CLIVE. All right. Once upon a time there was a little girl who lived all by herself in a prison.

PAMELA. Why? What had she done?

CLIVE. Nothing: that's the whole point. They took away all her clothes and made her wear blankets instead.

WALTER *enters from the kitchen.*

WALTER. Mrs Harrington was asking for her handbag.

PAMELA. Here it is. (*Takes handbag from armchair and*

hands it to WALTER.) Stay with us. Clive's telling me a story.

WALTER. A story? About history?

PAMELA. About a prison.

CLIVE. (*Showing off to* WALTER.) Yes, it's going to be brilliant! All Gothic darkness and calamities. It's called the 'Black Hole of East Suffolk'. (*Mock grave.*) Sit down and I'll unfold.

WALTER. No, not now. Your mother is waiting. Excuse me. (*He goes back into the kitchen.*)

CLIVE *stares after* WALTER. *His gaiety leaves him.*

PAMELA. What's wrong?

CLIVE. Nothing. (*In an everyday voice, almost brusque.*) Come on. Let's get on with your history.

CURTAIN

ACT ONE

SCENE TWO

A Saturday night two months later.
  *The family has finished dinner and is taking coffee. At
  least* STANLEY *and* LOUISE *are:* CLIVE, *sitting by his
  mother, is drinking whisky. His suitcase stands by the door.*

LOUISE. (*To* CLIVE.) Don't you want any coffee?

CLIVE. No thanks.

LOUISE. What are you drinking?

CLIVE. Whisky.

LOUISE. Really, I do think you might have caught an
  earlier train from Cambridge. I cooked a special dinner
  for you, all your favourite things.

CLIVE. I'm sorry, Mother. But don't worry, I had a perfectly good sandwich from British Railways.

LOUISE. Well, that's not enough for you.

*The sound of piano practising comes from the music room: a
  simple piece of Bach being repeated with many mistakes and
  stumbles.* WALTER *comes in from the kitchen and is about
  to go on up to his room.*

STANLEY. (*Referring to piano practising.*) How much
  longer is that going on, may I ask?

LOUISE. For another half-hour I hope. (*To* WALTER.)
  How's she getting on, dear?

WALTER. Oh, very well, Mrs Harrington. (*To* STANLEY.)
  It is only six weeks, you know, sir.

LOUISE. Yes, it's amazing, isn't it? Oh, Walter, would
  you mind taking Clive's suitcase upstairs as you go?

WALTER. Certainly, Mrs Harrington. (*Exit.*)

LOUISE. Thank you so much. (*To* CLIVE.) I don't know why you can't put your own things away.

STANLEY. (*To* CLIVE.) And that's what you call great music? Is that right? Great music?

CLIVE. (*Nervously, with an attempt at humour.*) Let's say it's a little distorted at the moment.

STANLEY. Distorted? It's driving me mad.

CLIVE. I suppose we can't expect her to be an expert in two months. Run-before-you-can-walk Department.

LOUISE. Your father imagines that everything can be done without hard work. Everything except making money out of the furniture business. (*To* STANLEY.) Really you are absurd. How do you think Paderewski sounded when he was practising? What is that piece she's learning, dear? Mozart? . . . Jou-jou, I'm talking to you.

CLIVE. (*Low.*) Bach.

LOUISE. You could play too if you wanted to. You've got the hands for it.

LOUISE *goes out to kitchen.* CLIVE *smiles faintly. There is a pause. A passage is repeated on the piano several times. Then an irritated bang on the keys and the noise stops.*

STANLEY. (*Carefully to* CLIVE.) Do you remember when you came to the factory to fetch your allowance the day you went up to Cambridge?

CLIVE. Yes. . . .

STANLEY. Did you have a talk to my manager while you were waiting?

CLIVE. Did I, yes . . . I suppose I did.

STANLEY. Yes. Is it true you told him you thought the furniture we make was—what was it?—'shoddy and vulgar'? (*Pause.*) Well?

CLIVE. I think I said it—it lacked . . .

STANLEY. What?

CLIVE. Well, that it didn't use materials as well as it might. Wood, for example. (*He smiles hopefully.*)

STANLEY. And the design was shoddy and vulgar?

CLIVE. Well—well, yes, I suppose I gave that impression. Not all of it, of course—just some things . . .

STANLEY. What things?

CLIVE. (*Plucking up a little courage.*) Well, those terrible oak cupboards, for example. I think you call it the Jacobean line. And those three piece suites in mauve moquette. Things like that . . .

STANLEY. (*Impassive as ever.*) Mr Clark said you called them 'grotesque'.

CLIVE *lowers his eyes.*

Is that right—grotesque?

CLIVE. (*Mumbling.*) I think they are, rather.

STANLEY. And I suppose you think that's clever. That's being educated, I suppose; to go up to my manager in my own factory and tell him you think the stuff I'm turning out is shoddy and vulgar. . . . Is it?

LOUISE *has come back from the kitchen in time to hear this.*

LOUISE. Just because *you've* got no taste, it doesn't mean we all have to follow suit.

STANLEY *gives her a look which silences her, then turns again to his son.* CLIVE *continues to sit rigid.*

STANLEY. Now you listen to me. You get this through your head once and for all; I'm in business to make money. I give people what they want. I mean ordinary people. Maybe they haven't got such wonderful taste as you and your mother; perhaps they don't read such good books—what is it?—'Houses and Gardens'?—but they know what they want. If they didn't want it, they wouldn't buy it, and I'd be out of business. Before you start sneering again, my boy, just remember something —you've always had enough to eat.

The explosive opening of the Brahms Third Symphony is heard from WALTER'S *room.*

(*Looking up, dangerously.*) One stops, the other starts. I'm going out.

STANLEY *stands up.*

LOUISE. Where to—Mr Benton?

STANLEY. And if I am at least I can get·some peace there.

LOUISE. Ssh.

STANLEY. Don't you ssh me!

LOUISE. This is the first week-end we've all been here together since Clive went up to Cambridge. I think the least you can do is stay home, his first evening back. Why must you be so disagreeable?

She goes into the hall calling 'Walter, Walter!'

WALTER. Did you call, Mrs Harrington?

LOUISE. Do you think you could play your gramophone another time, dear? Mr Harrington has got a slight headache.

WALTER. Of course, Mrs Harrington.

He goes into his room. Music stops, and he reappears.

I'm so sorry. So very sorry.

LOUISE. That's quite all right, dear. Thank you very much. I hate to disturb your concentration.

WALTER. Oh, please.

LOUISE. Come down when you want to. I've got some delicious petits-fours, and I'll make you some fresh coffee.

WALTER. Thank you, Mrs Harrington.

He goes into his room and shuts the door.

LOUISE. Now try and be a bit more agreeable will you? Jou-jou, it's washing-up time, are you going to help me?

CLIVE. Can't we leave it for once?

LOUISE. It's all right. I can manage perfectly well without you.

She goes into the kitchen. There is a silence.

CLIVE. I'm sorry I said that about the furniture, father. I suppose it was tactless of me.

STANLEY. Never mind. (*Pause.*) How are you doing at Cambridge? What about the other boys, do you get on with them?

CLIVE. (*Softly.*) It's not exactly like school you know. You rather pick your own friends.

STANLEY. Yes, I suppose you do. Well what do they do there? I mean apart from lessons.

CLIVE. Anything you like. There are all sorts of clubs and societies.

STANLEY. Do you belong to any?

CLIVE. Well, I joined a Dramatic Society as a matter of fact.

STANLEY. You mean for acting?

CLIVE. It's quite professional you know. They have their own theatre—and get reviews in *The Times*.

STANLEY. Don't any of them play any games?

CLIVE. Yes, but—well, the cricket and rugger are sort of professional standards. I thought of taking up fencing, it's not as odd as it sounds. It's meant to be very good for co-ordination——

STANLEY. What's that?

CLIVE. Muscles I think.

STANLEY. Clive, as you know your mother and I didn't see eye-to-eye over sending you to University. But that's past history now. The point is, what use are you going to make of it?

CLIVE. That's rather as it turns out, I should have thought. I mean you can't judge things in advance, can you?

STANLEY. Ah now that's just what I mean. Clive, if you don't know where you're going, you might as well pack up.

CLIVE. Why?

STANLEY. It's quite simple I should have thought.

CLIVE. It isn't. It just isn't like that. I mean if I knew where I was going I wouldn't have to go there, would I? I'd be there already.

STANLEY. What kind of silly quibble is that?

CLIVE. It's not a quibble. Look, education—being educated—you just can't talk about it in that way. It's something quite different—like setting off on an expedition into the jungle. Gradually most of the things you know disappear. The old birds fly out of the sky and new ones fly in you've never seen before. And everything surprises you too. Trees you expected to be just a few feet high grow right up over you—like the nave of Wells Cathedral. (*Suddenly embarrassed.*) Anyway if you had seen all this before, you wouldn't have to go looking. I think education is simply the process of being taken by surprise, don't you see?

STANLEY. Be that as it may.

CLIVE. You don't see.

STANLEY. Clive, I'm not talking about education. By all means, take advantage of your lessons. Look my boy, let's not pretend. Everyone doesn't get to Cambridge: you know it and I know it. You're in a privileged position and you must make the most of it. What you do now,

will influence the rest of your life. You know that, don't
you?

CLIVE. I suppose it will.

STANLEY. Of course it will. Take your friends for
example. What kind of friends do you have?

CLIVE. Do you want a list?

STANLEY. Now don't start getting on any high-horse.
I'm simply saying this. People still judge a man by the
company he keeps. You go around with a lot of drifters
and arty boys, and you'll be judged as one of them. I
don't say you do, and you're old enough to decide for
yourself anyway. Right?

CLIVE *nods*.

Number Two is this. Now's the time for you to be
making contacts with the right people. I mean people
who will be valuable to you later on. I don't mean the
smart people, or the fancy la-de-da people your mother's
always on about. I mean the people who really matter.
The people who have influence. Get in with them now,
and you won't go far wrong. I never had your advan-
tages. The contacts I made I had to work up myself.
So I know what I'm talking about. Do you understand?

CLIVE. Yes.

STANLEY. You've got a good brain and I'll see to it
you've got enough money. There's no harm in having a
few quid in your pocket you know.

LOUISE *enters*.

Don't ever be so stupid as to look down on money. It's
the one thing that counts in the end.

LOUISE. Money! Is that all you ever think about?

STANLEY. You don't have any difficulty spending it, I
notice. (*To* CLIVE.) Now let's see, how long have you
been at Cambridge? Is this your half-term holiday?

LOUISE. Half-term! You talk about it as if it were a grammar school, instead of our leading University. Really, Stanley, I don't know how one can even begin to talk to you.

STANLEY *stands up, furious, but trying to control himself.*

STANLEY. (*To* CLIVE.) Do you want to walk with me over to Benton's?

LOUISE *turns and stares at him in annoyance.*

CLIVE. I—I've got some reading to do actually.

STANLEY. We can stop in at the Lion for a quick one.

CLIVE. No. I don't think so really.

STANLEY. Very well.

CLIVE. It's important, or I would.

STANLEY *nods and goes out of the front door.* LOUISE *looks after him, then goes to her son.*

LOUISE. Are you going to be intense?

CLIVE. No.

LOUISE. Oh, Jou-jou! Mon petit Cossack. Embrasse-moi. . . . Non? . . . It's your Empress.

CLIVE. Your Majesty.

LOUISE. Every family has its rows you know. Come on, help me get the coffee—just the two of us.

CLIVE. In a moment, Mother.

LOUISE. All right, dear. But there's no need to take everything as if it were one of your Greek tragedies.

LOUISE *goes out into the kitchen.*

CLIVE *pours himself a drink.*

WALTER *comes out of his room down the stairs, knocks on the door and enters from the hall.*

WALTER. May I come in? I'm so sorry about the noise; if I had known I would not have played the machine.

CLIVE. Yes, it's a pity. Music always affects him that

way. The better the music the stronger the headache. Do you want a drink?

WALTER. No, thank you.

CLIVE. Was that the new record?

WALTER. (*Eagerly.*) Yes. It's what's called 'high fidelity'. You know—more bright and clear.

CLIVE. It sounds like the motto of a matrimonial agency. 'High Fidelity Guaranteed.'

WALTER. Splendid! It's nice to have you back, Clive. How are you finding Cambridge?

CLIVE. It's all right, I suppose.

WALTER. Is that all? Just all right?

CLIVE. (*Suddenly alive.*) No, it's wonderful! Like going to a new country. I suppose one of the thrills of travel is hearing people speak a foreign language. But the marvellous thing about this is, well, hearing them speak my own for the first time.

WALTER. I know.

CLIVE. Pam speaks a few words of it, of course, but it isn't quite enough. Where is she, by the way? Did she go for a walk?

WALTER. I think so, yes. It's a beautiful night.

CLIVE. Oh yes. A night for walks. Pam tripping along so gaily. Father marching along so . . . rightly. And I should be by his side. Or, better still, a pace or two behind. 'Clive, to heel, sir. Heel!' Let me introduce myself: 'Spaniel Harrington'. What's the matter?

WALTER. Nothing.

CLIVE. (*Mocking.*) Fathers should not be talked about like that . . . is that it?

WALTER. I think if you forgive me . . .

CLIVE. Well?

WALTER. You have a duty to your father.

CLIVE. Duty? What a very German thing to say. . . . Oh, that's terrible of me, isn't it? Forgive me, I'm not quite sober.

WALTER. I did not mean duty like that. I meant that it seems to me. . . . Clever children have a duty—to protect their parents who are not so clever.

CLIVE. Protect?

WALTER. I do not put it very well perhaps.

CLIVE. Walter, I want to . . .

LOUISE *enters from kitchen with a tray of coffee.*

LOUISE. Hibou! I'm so sorry about the gramophone.

WALTER. (*Recovering.*) Oh, it's me to be sorry . . . How is Mr Harrington?

LOUISE. It's nothing serious, my dear. He's gone out to clear his head. Well now, we seem to have the house to ourselves. What are we going to do? I know! Walter shall recite some beautiful poetry for us in German.

CLIVE. You don't understand German.

LOUISE. It's not the meaning, it's the sound that counts, dear. And I'm sure this boy will speak it adorably. Most people make it sound like a soda syphon, but when you speak it I'm sure I'll feel exactly what the poet wanted to say—even more than if I actually knew the language and to cope with all those millers' daughters and wood-cutters, and people. It's difficult to explain—but you know what I mean.

CLIVE. I don't. I'm going out.

LOUISE. Where?

CLIVE. To the pub.

LOUISE. You can't be serious.

CLIVE. Too vulgar?

LOUISE. Don't be silly, Clive. No, it's just so . . . uncivil, dear. There's plenty of drink in the house if you really

need it, though I think you've had quite enough
already.

CLIVE. (*Gravely.*) You're right, I have. (*To* WALTER.)
Excuse me. I'm sure you recite beautifully. (*He makes
for the french window.*)

LOUISE. (*With a resurgency of desperation.*) But your father
asked you if you wanted to go to the pub and you said
no.

CLIVE. True.

He goes out. WALTER *stands stiffly, very uncomfortable.*

LOUISE. Poor boy. I'm afraid he gets very upset down
here. He's essentially a town person really, like me.
And I get it from my mother. Being French, of
course.

*She wanders to the sofa, turning off the lamp, so that only the
standard and a table lamp remain on, creating a warmer
atmosphere.*

Like all Parisians she detested the country. She used
to say: 'Fields are for cows, drawing-rooms are for
ladies.' Of course it sounds better in French. (*She sits on
the sofa.*) What's the matter? Are you upset too? Oh,
Hibou. . . .

WALTER. It is nothing.

LOUISE. (*Semi-humorously.*) It is something . . . . Has
Clive been teasing you? He can be very naughty.

WALTER. I think he is not very happy.

LOUISE. He gets that from me, too.

WALTER. (*Sitting: impulsively.*) Mrs Harrington—is there
any help I can give? Anything at all?

LOUISE. I'm not a very happy person either, you know . . .
Well, you can see for yourself. (*Brightly.*) Whatever
you do, my dear boy, marry a girl who's your equal. If
you can find one. I'm sure it'll be hard! You see when I

married I was a very young girl. Believe it or not, I had hardly met anybody outside Bournemouth. My parents didn't consider it proper for me to run about on my own. And when I met Stanley they did everything in their power to arrange a marriage. You see, they weren't exactly very dependable people. My mother was an aristocratic little lady from France who'd never learnt to do a thing for herself all her life. My father was equally irresponsible: far too imaginative to make a good solicitor. And when he actually inherited a little money, he lost it all in speculation. 'Spec-u-lation'. Do you understand, dear?

WALTER. Oh, yes.

LOUISE. Your vocabulary's really amazing. Would you like a cigarette?

WALTER. Thank you, yes. (*He takes it awkwardly.*)

LOUISE. There. Where was I? Oh yes, my parents. Well, they acted in my best interests: I'm sure that's how they saw it. They wanted me to have all the comforts they couldn't give me themselves. . . . (*She warms her hands by the fire.*) Father kept saying it was a—what was the word?—a solid match. That's it. Stan the Solid: that's what I used to call him—as a joke, of course. And really a bit of admiration too, because my family was—well, so *liquid*, if you like. Just the opposite, anyway. No one ever worked consistently or made out budgets. So you see, the man had his fascination. Naturally, father had reservations about the marriage. I mean socially the thing was far from ideal—as I'm sure you realize. His people had always been professional men. Marrying me into the furniture business—(*with a faint smile*)—well, it was rather like going into trade in the old days. Still, I was rather attracted to Stanley. I won't deny it. He had a sort of rugged charm. He was born with nothing, of course, practically an orphan as well. His mother died in childbirth and his father was in the Merchant Navy. I gather he had a frightful time as a boy—but I will say this: it never showed in his manners. He was always terribly polite. Obviously I was interested in all sorts of things like art and music and poetry which he'd never had time for. But when you're young, things like that don't seem to matter. It's only later—when the first excitement's gone—you start looking a little closer. . . . (*With desperate seriousness; all trace of lightness suddenly going.*) Walter, these last few years have been intolerable. There are times when I listen to you playing; when I go almost mad with sheer pleasure. And yet year after year I've had to kill that side of myself, smother it, stamp it out. . . . Heaven knows, I've tried to be interested in his bridge and his golf club, and his terrible friends. I just can't do it. . . . (*Intimately.*) You know, don't you? You of all people must know.

WALTER *looks down in embarrassment.*

I'm sorry. I didn't mean to talk like this. I'm embarrassing you.

WALTER. No.

LOUISE. (*Lightly.*) I'm being vulgar, aren't I?

WALTER. You could never be.

LOUISE. Dear Hibou . . . you understand—you understand why I'm still here. The children. At least I could see that *they* weren't stifled too. . . .

As he still sits with his head lowered:

Do you condemn me?

WALTER. How could I condemn—in your house?

LOUISE. (*Wryly.*) I think we can leave hospitality to one side.

WALTER. (*Pursuing his own thought.*) In the house you have given me also to live in, so I can sit here by a fire and talk, as if always I had had the right.

LOUISE. (*Sympathetically.*) Walter . . .

WALTER. Where I worked before I taught the children for two or three hours, and then was paid by their mothers, and back always to my small room—(*a faint smile*)—with my cooking, which is not so good. You will never know how much I owe to you.

LOUISE. My dear boy. . . . Tell me about your family. Your people in Germany.

WALTER *stiffens perceptibly into withdrawal.*

WALTER. There is nothing to tell.

LOUISE. There must be something.

WALTER. I was an orphan. Like Mr Harrington. My parents died when I was too young to remember them. I was brought up by my uncle and his wife.

LOUISE. Were they good to you?

WALTER. (*Non-committal.*) Very good, yes.

LOUISE. And—that's all you want to say?

WALTER. There is nothing else.

LOUISE. Don't think I'm being inquisitive. . . . It's only that you've come to mean so much to us all in such a very short time. You know that.

WALTER. I do not deserve it.

LOUISE. (*Warmly.*) You deserve far more. Far, far more. I knew as soon as I saw you at that terrible cocktail party in Knightsbridge, standing all by yourself in the corner pretending to study the pictures. Do you remember—before even I spoke to you I knew you were something quite exceptional. I remember thinking: such delicate hands . . . and that fair hair—(*touching it*) —it's the hair of a poet. He'll have a soft voice that

stammers a little from nervousness, and a lovely
Viennese accent . . .

WALTER. (*Stiffly.*) I am not Viennese, you know. I am
German.

LOUISE. Well, it's not so very different . . .

WALTER. (*Dogged.*) I am German. This is not so poetic . . .
even the name . . . I hate.

LOUISE. (*A little intimidated by the darkness in him.*) But
Hibou, there's good and bad in all countries—surely?

WALTER. (*Gently.*) You are too good to understand what
I mean. I know how they seem to you, the Germans: so
kind and quaint. Like you yourself said: millers'
daughters and woodcutters. . . . But they can be
monsters.

LOUISE. (*Prepared to mock him.*) Really now——

WALTER. Yes! . . .

He gets up sharply and moves away. He is plainly distressed.
LOUISE *looks at him curiously.*

LOUISE. You know, even in England, we're not all angels.

WALTER. Yes, angels to me! Because this to me is
Paradise.

LOUISE. How charming you are.

WALTER. (*With increasing heat.*) No, I am sincere. Here in
England most people *want* to do what's good. Where I
was born this is not true. They want only power. . . .
They are a people that is enraged by equality. It needs
always to be ashamed, to breathe in shame—like oxygen
—to go on living. Because deeper than everything else
they want to be hated. From this they can believe they
are giants, even in chains. . . . (*Recovering.*) I'm sorry.
It's difficult to talk about.

LOUISE. Anything one feels deeply about is hard to speak
of, my dear.

WALTER. One thing I know: I will never go back. Soon I'll be a British subject.

LOUISE. You really want to stay here.

WALTER. If you had seen what I have, you would know why I call it Paradise.

LOUISE. I can see for myself how you've suffered. It's in your face. . . . (*Extending her hand to him.*) Walter . . .

He approaches her slowly, takes her hand, and sits down beside her again. He is still plainly upset. LOUISE *speaks very calmly.* You mustn't torment yourself like this. It's not good for you. You're among friends now. People who want to help you. People who love you. . . . Doesn't that make a difference?

Impulsively he bends and kisses her hands.

WALTER. You are so good! So good, good. . . .

Suddenly she takes his head in her hands and holds it close to her.

LOUISE. (*Tenderly.*) Oh, my dear . . . you make me feel ashamed.

CLIVE *comes abruptly in through the french window. He stares at them fascinated.*

It's been so long since anyone has said things like this to me.

CLIVE *bangs a chair hard against the table.*

Jou-jou!

She rises and tries to recover her composure.

Have you had a nice walk? Did you see Pam?

CLIVE *remains where he is, still staring at his mother.*

You know, it's absurdly late for her to be walking alone. Are you sure you didn't see her? She's probably gone over to that dreadful friend of hers, Mary whatever-her-name-is. I think it's high time she found another friend, don't you?

As CLIVE *goes on staring, her last remnant of poise deserts her.*

Perhaps she's upstairs after all. She may have come in by the front door. I'll just go up and see . . .

She leaves the room and goes quickly upstairs to her own room. All the while the two boys have stayed quite still, WALTER *on the sofa,* CLIVE *by the door. Now* CLIVE *goes slowly over to* WALTER *and fingers his dishevelled hair. He is evidently fairly drunk, but alcohol does not impair his speech. Rather it gives it energy and turns of speed. Now he is more disturbed than he himself is aware.*

WALTER. Clive, what is the matter? Why are you looking at me like that?

CLIVE. Hair is being worn dishevelled this year. The Medusa style. What would have happened if Medusa had looked in a mirror? Are monsters immune against their own fatal charms? . . . Observe, please, the suble and dialectical nature of my mind. It's the French in me, you understand. An inheritance from my very French, very aristocratic ancestors. Perhaps you've been hearing about them. In reality, I regret to say, they weren't as aristocratic as all that. My great-grandpa, despite any impression to the contrary, did not actually grant humble petitions from his bedside:—merely industrial patents from a run-down little office near the Louvre. The salary was so small that the family would have died of starvation if Hélène, my grandmother, hadn't met an English solicitor—on a cycling tour of the Loire— married him, and exchanged Brunoy for Bournemouth. Let us therefore not gasp too excitedly at the loftiness of Mother's family tree. Unbeknown to Father, it has, as you see, roots of clay. Still, they *are* French roots. I even have them in me. For example—my Mother's name for me—Jou-jou. Toy. More accurately in this case, ornament.

WALTER *remains silent. As he talks on, with increasing bitterness,* CLIVE *wanders aimlessly round the room.*

Being French, you know, Mother imagines she's real ormolu in a sitting-room of plaster gilt. She suffers from what I might call a plaster-gilt complex, if you see what I mean. To her the whole world is irredeemably plebeian—especially Father. The rift you may detect between them is the difference between the Salon and the Saloon. At least that's what she'd have you believe . . . I won't deny that she's only really at home in the Salon; but then where else can you be so continuously dishonest?

WALTER. (*Stung into speech.*) Please——

CLIVE. Yes?

WALTER. I do not wish to hear this. It's not right.

CLIVE. Ah—you do not wish! The young *charming* tutor does not wish. . . . So delicate, so old-world! A tutor and his employer by the fireside. Paris calling to Vienna. The waltz plays on the deserted boulevard: Europe crumbles. Oh, the *charm* of it! . . . Do let's salvage what we can. If we can't have a château in Brittany, then we *can* have a country place in Suffolk, which is almost as desolate but rather more convenient. If we can't install scholars in our library, because we haven't got a library, since nobody reads in our house, why then the least we can do is get in a dear gentle tutor for the girl. Someone with tone, of course; nothing grubby from the Polytechnic. . . . You see, we're specialists in delicacy.

WALTER. I do not understand you.

CLIVE. What; our delicacy?

WALTER. Why you talk like this.

CLIVE. Because I'm not really so damned delicate after

all. Because actually, if you want to know, I'm getting less bloody delicate all the time.

WALTER. (*Rising.*) I do not think I can listen to any more.

CLIVE. Where are you going?

WALTER. If you had come from Europe, if you had been taken in, as I was—alone——

CLIVE. Taken in! Taken in is right!

WALTER. Excuse me.

CLIVE. (*Going after him.*) Or no—taken up! Like a fashion. Or an ornament; a piece of Dresden, a dear little Dresden owl.

He pushes him down into the armchair and leans over him, staring intensely into his face. A long pause. CLIVE becomes aware of his position and draws back a little.

And believe me, love, sooner or later, like any other valuable possession, you will be used. I know this family, let me tell you. If you can't help one of us score a point over the others—you've no claim on our notice. Oh, my dear fellow——

The front door slams. PAMELA comes in and runs upstairs.

LOUISE. (*Calling.*) Pam, is that you?

She appears on the landing. CLIVE opens the door and stands in an attitude of listening, stock-still. WALTER watches him uncertainly.

PAMELA. (*Breathlessly.*) Yes. It's all me!

LOUISE. It's rather late, dear. I wish you'd take your walks earlier.

PAMELA. (*Taking off her coat.*) I'm sorry.

LOUISE. Where did you go?

PAMELA. Over to Mary's. You know, she is the absolute best: she tells the funniest stories in the world. D'you know what happened? Last week Ted—that's her brother

—took his daughter to the ballet. She's just eight, and it was a sort of extra birthday present. Well, she watched all these girls going up on their toes—(*illustrates*)—and dancing about—and you know what she said at the end? 'Daddy, why don't they just get taller girls?' (LOUISE *is unamused.*) Don't you think that's funny?

LOUISE. Yes dear, very funny. (*She kisses her daughter.*) Good night, dear.

PAMELA. Good night, mother.

She goes into the schoolroom and then into her own room, closing the door. LOUISE *looks after her for a moment, then returns to her room.* CLIVE *closes the door again.*

CLIVE. (*Keeping still and quiet: to himself.*) Hepcat! She's the only one who's free, with her private star of Grace . . . . It's a marvellous dispensation: to escape one's inheritance. (*To* WALTER.) I don't mean you. . . . Walter, you're one of the best people who ever came into our house. You think I don't know how lonely you were before you came here. You're wrong. I can smell your loneliness. . . . You see, I've only one real talent; being able to see what's true, and just what isn't. And that's an awful thing to have. (*With sudden animation.*) Come away with me.

WALTER. (*Startled.*) What? Come away?

CLIVE. Look—in four weeks my term ends. We could go somewhere; to the West Country if you like. Wells Cathedral is the most astonishing thing in England. It's like walking down the throat of a whale: a skeleton whale, with the vertebrae showing. No one will be there at Christmas. Cheddar Gorge without a single charabanc! That's a bus, you know. . . .

WALTER. Yes, I know!

CLIVE. Please say yes. . . . You'd love it.

WALTER. (*With a shy smile.*) I'm sorry. Christmas is a family time. For so long I have missed it. This year I wish very much to pass it here.

CLIVE. (*Insistently.*) Well, afterwards. I could wait.

WALTER. (*Awkwardly: his whole stance awkward.*) I'm afraid it's not possible. My lessons, you see. I have been paid already to the end of January.

CLIVE. So what? Everyone takes Christmas off.

WALTER. I do not think I can go away just now.

CLIVE. Because you've been paid?

WALTER. No. . . .

CLIVE. Then why?

WALTER. I—I have an obligation.

CLIVE. To my mother?

WALTER. Yes. An obligation.

CLIVE. Is that what you call it—obligation? Well, doff my plumed hat! Gallant Walter Langer. . . . The Cavalier Tutor to his Mistress! Or do I mean the Cavalier Teuton? . . . Don't look so startled. Proper cavaliers have only figurative mistresses.

He turns away, swept into frantic remorse. As before, he holds himself very stiffly.

This is quite beyond anything, isn't it? (*With the quietness of desperation.*) If you came away with me, it would be for my sake—not yours. I need a friend so badly.

WALTER. (*As stiff himself.*) You are unhappy. I am sorry.

CLIVE. (*The bitterness returning.*) Is that all you can say? 'I'm sorry'. 'I regret'. Such an awkward position I put you in, don't I? The poor little immigrant, careful not to offend. So very sensitive. (*With sudden fury.*) When in hell are you going to stop trading on your helplessness—offering yourself all day to be petted and stroked?

Yes, just like I do! O.K. you're a pet. You've got an irresistible accent. You make me sick.

WALTER. Excuse me.

He makes for the door. CLIVE *seeks to detain him, clumsily.*

CLIVE. Walter, Walter, I didn't—please——

WALTER *leaves the room and goes up to his own.* CLIVE *stands looking at the closed door.*

CLIVE. (*Dully.*) Please!

Slowly he turns away from it and goes eventually to the bottle of whisky. WALTER *reaches the landing.* PAMELA *comes out of her room in her nightdress, on her way to the bathroom.*

PAMELA. Hullo? Oh, it's you.

WALTER. Yes.

PAMELA. Is there anything wrong?

WALTER. No.

PAMELA. You look as if they were going to cut off your head in the morning.

WALTER. (*Smiling, with effort.*) Do I? . . . You were walking?

PAMELA. Yes. Mary and I discovered a new place in the woods, with a huge stream you can dam up. I don't suppose it's anything compared with your river, the one you could skate on.

WALTER. You show it to me tomorrow.

PAMELA. Yes. (*Pulling out her nightdress.*) Are you shocked because I'm in my this?

WALTER. Yes. Very.

PAMELA. Then you'd better leave, sir. I'm on my way to the bathroom and I've no wish to cause you embarrassment.

He bows. She curtsies.

Good night.

WALTER. Good night.

He goes into his own room and shuts the door. She looks after him for a second and blows him a kiss before passing on to her bath.

Downstairs CLIVE *is pouring out another drink.* STANLEY *comes in through the front door, takes off his overcoat, hangs it up in the hall and comes into the living-room.* CLIVE *puts down the glass guiltily.*

STANLEY. What are you doing?

CLIVE. Stealing your drink.

STANLEY. You don't have to steal from me, Clive. You're old enough to take a drink if you want one. Where's your mother?

CLIVE. I don't know—upstairs. . . .

STANLEY. (*Expansively.*) You ought to have come with me to Benton's. We went over to the Club. Jolly nice crowd there. The sort of fellows *you* ought to be mixing with. There was a chap there in publishing. You'd have been interested. . . . (*Pause.*) Clive, I've told you before, in this world you want to get in with the people who matter. But you've got to make an effort, my boy. Make yourself a bit popular. You see? And you're not going to do that sitting here drinking by yourself. Are you?

CLIVE. (*Low.*) No, I suppose not.

STANLEY. What d'you want to do it for anyway?

CLIVE. (*Shrugging.*) I don't know.

STANLEY. Well, it's damn' silly and it's not normal. If you want to drink—drink with others. Everyone likes a drink. You come over to the Club with me, you'll soon find that out. I'll make you a member. You'll get in with them in a jiffy if you'll only try.

CLIVE. Yes. (*Pause.*) Well . . . I think I'll go to bed now.

STANLEY. (*As* CLIVE *makes for the door.*) Just a minute.

What's the matter? Aren't they good enough for you? Is that it?

CLIVE. (*Gently.*) No, of course it isn't.

STANLEY. Then what?

CLIVE. (*Gaining courage.*) Well, all this stuff—right people, wrong people—people who Matter. It's all so meaningless.

STANLEY. It's not a bit meaningless.

CLIVE. Well, all right, they matter! But what can I say to them if they don't matter to *me*? Look, you just can't talk about people in that way. It's unreal—idiotic. As far as I'm concerned one of the few people who really matters to me in Cambridge is an Indian.

STANLEY. Well, there's nothing wrong in that. What's his father? A rajah or something?

CLIVE. His father runs a cake shop in Bombay.

STANLEY. Well, what sort of boy is he? What's he like?

CLIVE. He's completely still. . . I don't mean he doesn't move. I mean that deep down inside him there's a sort of happy stillness, that makes all our family rows and raised voices here seem like a kind of—blasphemy almost. That's why he matters—because he loves living so much. Because he understands birds and makes shadow puppets out of cardboard, and loves Ella Fitzgerald, and Vivaldi, and Lewis Carroll; and because he plays chess like a devil and makes the best prawn curry in the world. And this is him. Well, parts of him. Bits of him.

STANLEY. (*Bewildered and impatient.*) Well, of course I'm glad you've got some nice friends.

CLIVE. (*Sharp.*) Don't. Don't do that.

STANLEY. What?

CLIVE. Patronize. It's just too much.

STANLEY. I'm not patronizing you, Clive.

CLIVE. Oh yes, you are. That's precisely what you're doing.

STANLEY. That's very unfair.

CLIVE. (*Working himself into a deep rage.*) Precisely. Precisely! 'I'm very glad you have some nice chums, Clive. I did too at your age.' . . . These aren't my little play-pals, Father. They're important people. Important to me.

STANLEY. Did I say they weren't?

PAMELA *returns from the bath. She listens for a brief moment in the schoolroom to her brother's raised voice, then goes on into her room.*

CLIVE. (*Frantic.*) Important! It is important they should be alive. Every person they meet should be altered by them, or at least remember them with terrific—terrific excitement. That's an important person. Can't you understand?

STANLEY. (*Crushingly.*) No, Clive. I'm afraid I don't. I don't understand you at all.

A slight pause. CLIVE *subsides. When he speaks again it is to renew the attack in a colder and more accusing voice.*

CLIVE. You're proud of it too.

STANLEY. (*Getting angry.*) What now?

CLIVE. That you don't understand me at all. Almost as if it defined you. 'I'm the Man Who Doesn't Understand!' (*Furiously.*) Has it ever occurred to you that *I* don't understand *you?* No. Of course not! Because you're the one who does the understanding around here—or rather, fails to. What work did you ever put in to be able to understand anybody?

STANLEY. I think you'd better go to bed.

For a moment CLIVE *seems ready to obey. Then:*

CLIVE. I'll go to bed when I'm good and ready! . . . D'you think it falls into your lap—some sort of a grace that enters you when you become a father?

STANLEY. You're drunk.

CLIVE. Yes, you think you can treat me like a child! But *you* don't even know the right way to treat a child. Because a child is private and important and *itself*. Not an extension of you, any more than I am.

He falls quiet, dead quiet—as if explaining something very difficult. His speech slows and his face betrays an almost obsessed sincerity as he sits.

I am myself. Myself. Myself. You think of me only as what I might become. What I might make of myself. But I am myself now—with every breath I take, every blink of the eyelash. The taste of a chestnut or a strawberry on my tongue is me. The smell of my skin is me. The trees and sofas that I see with my own eyes are me. And you should want to become me and see them as I see them. But we can never exchange. Feelings don't *unite* us, don't you see? They keep us apart. And words don't help because they're unreal. We live away in our skins from minute to minute, feeling everything quite differently, and any one minute's just as true about us as any other. Yes, I'm drunk. You make me drunk.

Pause.

STANLEY. I do?

CLIVE. (*Losing heart.*) You and everything. . . .

STANLEY. What are you talking about?

CLIVE. Nothing. It doesn't matter. Everything stays as it is.

STANLEY. Well——

CLIVE. (*With a final spurt of energy.*) I'm talking about

care. Taking care. Care of people you want to know. Not just doing your best for them, and hoping the best for them. I mean you've got to care for them *as they are*, from blink to blink. . . . Don't you see? The—the renewing of your cells every day makes you a sacred object, or it should do, in the eyes of people who care for you. It's far more important than whether you speculate in fish or furniture. Because what you do in the world and so on isn't important at all, not in the slightest, compared with what you look like and sound like and feel like as the minutes go by. That's why a question like 'What are you going to be?' is quite unreal. Do you see?

A long pause.

STANLEY. Well, that's given me something to think about, old boy. Why don't we go on with it in the morning? What?

CLIVE *does not reply.* STANLEY *goes to the door.*

Good night, then. . . . I said good night, Clive.

Still CLIVE *takes no notice.* STANLEY *shrugs and leaves the room, turning out the lights, so that only the glow of the fire and one lamp remain. He goes slowly upstairs.*

For a moment CLIVE *remains where he is, in a trance of private depression. Then slowly he rises and crosses to the sofa. On the coffee table are* WALTER'S *spectacles in their case. He picks them up and takes them out. He begins to cry, terribly, almost silently. Up on the landing* STANLEY *hesitates, conscious of his failure. He shakes his head and returns on impulse downstairs.*

Don't forget to turn off the fire. . . .

CLIVE *makes an effort to control himself and fails.* STANLEY *goes to him.*

STANLEY. What is it, boy? What's the matter?

CLIVE *shakes his head 'No'.*

What? Come on, now. Out with it. What's the matter—can't you tell me? That's a silly attitude to take, isn't it? After all, I'm your father. It's what I'm here for.

CLIVE *shies away from the thought of contact as* STANLEY *makes to touch his arm.*

Here! There's something really wrong, isn't there?

CLIVE.(*Whispering.*) No.

STANLEY. Something's happened.

CLIVE. No. . . .

STANLEY. When?

CLIVE *goes on shaking his head.*

While I was out? That's it, isn't it? While I was out.

CLIVE. No!

STANLEY. What was it? Did your mother say something? (*He sees the spectacles.*) Was it something to do with Walter? Yes!

He snatches the spectacles as CLIVE *breaks free from him and moves sharply away.*

That's it, isn't it? Well, what? What happened with Walter?

CLIVE. (*Frightened.*) I don't know. I don't know.

STANLEY. (*Relentlessly.*) What happened with Walter? Answer me!

CLIVE *bolts away to the door, then suddenly he changes his mind, closes it, comes back into the room and faces his father.*

CLIVE. (*Very quiet.*) It was mother.

STANLEY. What?

CLIVE. There on the sofa. I saw them. I came in and there they were. The light was turned down. They were kissing. *Kissing!* She was half undressed, and he was kissing her, on the mouth. On the breasts. Kissing . . .

STANLEY *hits him. He falls on the sofa.*
  (*Hard.*) And before that, I think the light had been turned off.
STANLEY *stares at him, stunned. Nervelessly he drops the spectacles into the armchair.*
  Department of Just Deserts?

CURTAIN

ACT TWO

The following morning. Sunday. A bright, cold day.

WALTER *and* PAMELA *are sitting at the breakfast table. The girl, in her dressing-gown, is reading one of the better Sunday papers.*

PAMELA. Walter, what does 'Salacious' mean?

WALTER. What word?

PAMELA. Salacious—it's in this article.

WALTER. Show me. (*Takes paper.*) Where are my glasses? (*He sees them in the armchair where* STANLEY *dropped them the night before.*) Ah. Now. Salacious. . . . Yes. It means 'wise'.

PAMELA. Does it? I suppose I should have guessed. You ought to teach English.

WALTER. I wouldn't dare.

PAMELA. Oh, phooey. I'm sure you'd be miles better than the man at my last school. Anyway, he was a Dutchman. (*Taking back the paper.*) Mother says this is the only Sunday paper she'll have in the house. I think it's mean of her. Everyone else has the popular ones with pictures of rapes. . . .

LOUISE *comes in with a tray from the kitchen.* WALTER *immediately stands.*

LOUISE. Did you enjoy the kippers?

WALTER. Yes, they were splendid, thank you.

LOUISE. Do sit down, my dear.

He does so.

PAMELA. Mother, why can't we have Sunday papers with sexy pictures in?

LOUISE. (*Loading the tray with used plates.*) Because they're vulgar, and give you a distorted view of life.

PAMELA. I don't mind.

LOUISE. Well, I do. Where's Clive?

PAMELA. Not down yet.

LOUISE. Really, you children are the limit. I just don't see why you can't all have your breakfast together. It's late enough, heaven knows. (*Lifting the tray.*) Pamela, you'd better hurry up and finish dressing if you're going riding.

She goes back to the kitchen, WALTER *holding open the door for her.*

PAMELA. Have you ever gone riding?

WALTER. (*Coming back to the table and sitting.*) No.

PAMELA. It's the best, absolutely. What games did you play in Germany?

WALTER. I—I used to walk.

PAMELA. You mean on hiking parties, all dressed up in those leather shorts?

WALTER. No. By myself. I liked it better.

PAMELA. (*Impulsively.*) Are you happy here? Are you really, really happy?

WALTER. Of course.

PAMELA. Who do you like best?

WALTER. You.

PAMELA. No, seriously.

WALTER. I like you all. You and your mother . . .

PAMELA. And Clive?

WALTER. Of course and Clive. I like him very much. I'm only sorry he is so unhappy.

PAMELA. Is he very unhappy?

WALTER. I think so, yes.

PAMELA. That's because he was spoilt when he was young.

WALTER. Spoilt?

PAMELA. You know—to spoil someone. Like damage.

WALTER. Oh, damage: yes! . . .

PAMELA. (*Downright; drinking her coffee.*) I'm sure he ought to get married.

WALTER. Oh, he's so young!

PAMELA. For some people it's the best thing. You must help him find a girl.

WALTER. Has he not had friendships with girls before?

PAMELA. (*In her 'affected' voice.*) Not even acquaintance-ships, my dear. (*Normal.*) Except one; a girl called Peggy-Ann who worked in the tobacconist's when we were in the Isle of Wight. She used to wear leopard skin trousers and great sort of brass bells in her ears. Clive said they used to go down on the beach and neck, but I bet he was just bragging. So you see, you've got to help him. I'm sure you know hundreds of girls.

WALTER. (*Amused.*) Oh, yes. What kind would you suggest?

PAMELA. Someone who'll pay him lots of attention. At home, everyone keeps on at him but no one really takes any notice of him. (*Brightly.*) Clive spends his whole time not being listened to.

WALTER. His mother listens, doesn't she?

PAMELA. Not really listens, no. . . . Well of course you can't expect her to. No mother ever really listens to her children. It's not done.

WALTER. You seem to know a lot about it.

PAMELA. Yes, I do. Poor Clive. You know, they really

only use him to help them when they're rowing.
(*Directly.*) Can you understand why they row?

WALTER. I think everyone has quarrels.

PAMELA. Yes, but this is different. With Mother and
Daddy the row is never really *about*—well, what they're
quarrelling about. I mean . . . behind what they say you
can feel—well, that Mother did this in the past, and
Daddy did that. I don't mean anything *particular* . . .
(*She stops, confused.*) Oh, dear . . . I think marriage is a
very difficult subject, don't you?

WALTER. (*Humorously; he is a little uncomfortable.*) You
don't take your exam in it till you're a little older.

PAMELA. (*Pursuing her own thought.*) I mean, who begins
things? Do you see?

WALTER. Please, Pamela——

PAMELA. I know Mother's frightful to him about culture,
and uses music and things to keep him out—which is
terrible. But isn't that just because *he* made *her* keep out
of things when they were first married? You know he
wouldn't even let her go to concerts and theatres
although she was dying to, and once he threw a picture
she'd bought into the dustbin; one of those modern
things, all squiggles and blobs. (*Gestures.*) . . . But then,
mightn't *that* just have been because being brought up
by himself he was afraid of making a fool of himself. Oh,
poor Daddy . . . Poor Mother, too. (*To him, brightly.*)
You know, I shouldn't wonder if parents don't turn out
to be my hobby when I grow up.

STANLEY *appears on the landing and descends the stairs.*

WALTER. (*Warmly.*) You have a wonderful mother, you
know.

PAMELA. Yes, I suppose so.

WALTER. Only suppose?

PAMELA. People who make you feel stupid are always called wonderful.

STANLEY *comes into the living-room. He looks tired and strained.*

Good morning, Daddy.

STANLEY. (*Kissing her.*) Morning, dear.

He stares at WALTER *with a curious unwilling stare.* WALTER *rises rather awkwardly.*

WALTER. Good morning, sir.

PAMELA. What's wrong? Aren't you feeling well?

He looks at her fixedly, almost unseeingly; then sits slowly down at the table. LOUISE *comes in from the kitchen, wearing an apron.*

LOUISE. Stanley. . . ? (*Entering.*) You might let me know when you come down. Walter dear, will you come and get Mr Harrington's cereal for me?

WALTER. (*Eager to help.*) Of course, Mrs Harrington.

She goes into the kitchen again.

I hope your headache is better this morning, sir.

He exits to kitchen. STANLEY *nods, apparently unable to speak.*

PAMELA. You aren't wearing your lovely coat.

STANLEY. No. I'm not going shooting today, darling, it's Sunday.

PAMELA. Well, come riding with me, then.

STANLEY. (*Wrapped in himself.*) No. . . . Not today. I . . . just want to take things quiet.

PAMELA. (*Mischievously.*) You're getting old.

He looks at her searchingly.

STANLEY. Why don't you ever learn to tie that ribbon? Come here.

She inclines her head. He fixes the ribbon.

Has Clive come down yet?

PAMELA. No, the lazy pig. You were talking to him late last night, weren't you? I could hear you from upstairs. Well, really, it seemed more like Clive was talking to you.

WALTER *reappears, smiling, with porridge, a napkin over his arm.*

WALTER. (*Placing it smartly before* STANLEY *and acting the waiter for* PAMELA *behind his back.*) Mrs Harrington asks would you prefer eggs or kippers?

STANLEY. (*Quietly.*) Nothing.

PAMELA. Daddy, you must have something.

STANLEY. Don't fuss, Pam, please. (*Curtly, to* WALTER.) Nothing.

WALTER. (*With a half bow.*) Yes, sir.

He goes back to the kitchen, deflated, his smile gone.

PAMELA. He'd make a wonderful waiter, wouldn't he? How did you like Clive talking to you man to man? (*Brightly.*) He must have been drunk.

STANLEY. Why do you say that?

PAMELA. Because if he wasn't, he never would have. Not properly, anyway. He'd be too nervous.

He looks at her sharply.

That's because you like him to answer questions all the time, and he hates to.

STANLEY. Why?

PAMELA. I don't know. I suppose he's just not the answering type. D'you know he even has a dream about you?

STANLEY. Clive?

PAMELA. Yes. He gets it quite often, so he must think an awful lot about you. You ought to be flattered, though it's not exactly what I'd call a flattering dream . . . (*Recounting it carefully, with increasing drama.*) Apparently, he's always in bed lying down under thick blankets. Near him is a window and he can see into a big garden all covered in snow. It's freezing so hard he can hear twigs snapping on the trees. Then suddenly you appear, coming slowly over the snow towards him— crunch . . . crunch . . . crunch. You disappear inside the house and he can hear you coming upstairs—crunch . . . crunch . . . and along the passage to his bedroom. Then the door slowly opens and you come in, and cross the room to see if he's asleep. So while you stand there he pretends to be asleep as asleep can be, except that some- times he starts shivering, which spoils the effect. Then you start taking off the blankets one by one. Clive says there must be about ten blankets on the bed, and with each one you take off he gets colder and colder. Usually he wakes up with all his bedclothes on the floor. Isn't that the silliest dream you ever heard . . . ? I told him the next time he heard you coming upstairs he was to wait till you came up to the bed, then sit bolt upright and shout 'Go to hell!'

STANLEY *has listened to this impassively but with the greatest attention. He still sits involved in his own silent conflict as* LOUISE *returns from the kitchen.*

LOUISE. (*To* PAMELA.) Pamela! Are you still here? You're going to be very late for your ride. And I've told you before, unpunctuality is just bad breeding. (WALTER *enters.*)

PAMELA. (*To* WALTER.) I've decided you'd make the most wonderful waiter. . . .

LOUISE. (*Shocked.*) Pamela! What a thing to say.

PAMELA. Well, he would. Can't you just see him bowing to old ladies with Pekineses?

LOUISE. Stop it, Pamela. That's very rude. A waiter! Can't you think of anything else for Walter to be? I only hope one day you'll have a tiny part of his education, (*To* WALTER.) and a few of his manners. (*To* PAMELA.) Now hurry up and get dressed. (WALTER *goes out and upstairs into the schoolroom to get a book.*) Your picnic's all ready.

PAMELA. Daddy, can I borrow your red jacket? Please say yes.

STANLEY. (*Quiet.*) Of course—it'll be a bit big, though, won't it?

PAMELA. Nonsense—I shall wear it as a cape. Of course I won't look half so good in it as you do.

STANLEY. Enjoy the ride.

PAMELA. (*Intimately.*) You bet.

LOUISE. And tell Clive from me, if he's not down right away he won't get any breakfast.

PAMELA *goes out and upstairs, getting her riding-cap and crop from the hall as she passes.*

Stanley, what are you sitting there for? I hear you didn't want any cooked breakfast. And you haven't even touched your cereal. That's absurd. You must have something to eat. (*He stares now at her.*) What's the matter? Did you have too much to drink last night or something?

He rises and goes to the french window.

Stanley. . . .

Abruptly he goes into the garden. LOUISE *stares after him in astonishment. She sits down at the table.*

PAMELA *emerges on the landing.*

PAMELA. Walter?

WALTER. (*Coming from the schoolroom and joining her on the landing.*) Hallo?

PAMELA. I wasn't really rude just now, was I?

WALTER. No, of course not. As a matter of fact, I was a waiter once, for a short time in Berlin. But they threw me out.

PAMELA. Why?

WALTER. No dignity. That's what they said.

PAMELA. How ridiculous. You're the most dignified man I ever met. (*Running off to* CLIVE's *door and banging on it.*) Clive! Wake up, wake up, whoever you are! Into your slippers, go down for your kippers . . . ! Wake up, wake up——

She returns, carrying the hunting jacket; after a pause, CLIVE *follows, wearing sports coat and slacks. He is tousled and with a slight hangover. He bows, Oriental fashion.*

CLIVE. Good morning.

PAMELA. (*Bowing also; in the act at once.*) Salaams. A thousand welcomes, O handsome slave boy, mine eyes rejoice in the sight of you! Dance for me, my little pomegranate! Madden me with desire!

CLIVE. Drop dead! (*To* WALTER.) Good morning. (*To* PAMELA.) Get him to do it.

WALTER. Excuse me. I think I work a little. . . .

He dives into his room and slams the door.

CLIVE. Where is everybody?

PAMELA. Downstairs. You'd better go down.

CLIVE *groans.*

You look a bit green. Do you want a fizzy?

CLIVE. No, thanks.

PAMELA. Well, salaams.

CLIVE. Salaams.

She runs off into her room. CLIVE *goes slowly downstairs, where* LOUISE *still sits at the table. He is clearly reluctant to go.*

LOUISE. You slept late. Perhaps you had a little too much to drink last night, too.

He does not reply.

There's kippers or eggs.

CLIVE. No thank you. Is there any coffee?

LOUISE. Now what is this? First your father and now you.

CLIVE. Where is he?

LOUISE. Outside.

CLIVE. (*Perplexed.*) Where?

LOUISE. In the garden. Well—isn't he?

CLIVE. (*Looking out.*) Yes. He's sitting down under the apple tree.

LOUISE. *Sitting?* In this weather? Without an overcoat? He'll catch his death. Tell him to come in at once.

CLIVE. Perhaps he prefers it outside.

LOUISE. Don't be ridiculous, Clive. The man must be mad, sitting out there on a freezing morning like this. (*Advancing to the french window.*) What on earth he thinks he's doing, I can't imagine.

CLIVE. (*Sharply.*) Leave him alone!

LOUISE. (*Amazed.*) Are you talking to me?

CLIVE. (*Firmly; almost surprised at himself.*) Leave him alone.

LOUISE. Are you sure you're feeling all right?——

CLIVE. I—I'm sorry.

LOUISE. So you should be. That was very, very ill bred.

CLIVE. (*Whispering.*) Not really done?

LOUISE. Clive, I don't understand you this morning. I really don't.

He smiles, delighted, to himself.

CLIVE. (*French accent.*) Votre Majesté should not worry 'erself about eet. It makes, as the Eenglish say, no nevaire mind. My Empress!

*He extends his hand in salutation. His mother, made un-
certain by the mockery in his manner, warily allows her
own to be taken and kissed. At the same moment the warm
slow movement of the Brahms Symphony is heard from*
WALTER'S *room. Suddenly she draws him to her—he
allows himself to be drawn—and embraces him. A brief instant
of great intimacy recurs, as it happened in the first scene.*

LOUISE. Jou-jou . . . !

CLIVE. Maman . . . !

LOUISE. Mon petit Cossack. Mon petit, petit . . . Silly boy.

*She holds him tenderly, in the position of subservience he took
up before his Empress, only now very close to her. His back
is to the audience, and from his inclined posture she can
fondle his head.*

D'you think I'm so stupid I don't know what's wrong?
D'you think I can't see for myself . . . ? We're a little
bit jealous, aren't we?

He moves sharply, but she continues to hold him.

As if you didn't always come first. You know that.
Don't you?

He nods, stiff now with reluctance.

Then it's so ridiculous, isn't it, to be jealous? And of
whom? A poor lonely boy with no people of his own to
care for him, all by himself in a foreign country. Really,
Jou-jou, you ought to be ashamed. Let's say no more
about it. I want you always to be happy—remember?

He nods again.

There. (*She releases him.*) Now, let me cook you some
breakfast. You could eat an egg, couldn't you?

CLIVE. (*Low.*) I suppose so.

LOUISE. Good. Come on then. You finish your coffee
while I get started. (*She looks at him tenderly and kisses
him on the forehead.*) Silly . . .

She goes out into the kitchen.

CLIVE. (*With a sort of bitter disgust; to himself.*) On waves of sympathy. On waves . . . !

He rises, turns to clear the table—then glances through the window and bolts quickly for the kitchen door.

STANLEY *comes in from the garden. He stands irresolute, as if searching for something he cannot find, his eyes blank, his whole manner distracted. The Brahms Symphony plays on. Unseen,* CLIVE *watches him through the kitchen door. Then, suddenly, he leaves the room and the house, banging the front door behind him.*

The door of PAMELA'S *bedroom opens after a moment, and she comes into the schoolroom, dressed in riding clothes, the hunting jacket on her arm. She goes out of the schoolroom and starts downstairs with her picnic box and thermos. She misses her footing and falls in an undignified heap on the landing.*

PAMELA. Damn! Damn! Damn!

Music stops. WALTER *comes rushing out, startled by the great crash. At the same time,* LOUISE *appears at the kitchen door.*

LOUISE. (*Calling up.*) Pamela! Are you all right? What on earth's that noise?

WALTER. What's the matter, Pamela? I help you . . .

He helps her solicitously to her feet.

Are you hurt?

PAMELA. (*Indignant at being found like this.*) Of course not!

WALTER. What happened?

PAMELA. I tripped and fell. I knew I would.

LOUISE. (*Running upstairs.*) Pamela!

PAMELA. I'm all right—don't fuss, Mother. Anyone would think I was dying. (*Feeling her head.*) Ow!

WALTER. See? You bumped your head.

PAMELA. (*Witheringly*.) When you fall down, you must bump something. It's usual.

WALTER. I look.

PAMELA. No!

LOUISE *arrives on the landing*.

LOUISE. My darling, are you all right . . . ?

PAMELA. (*Cool.*) Perfectly, thank you.

WALTER. (*Concerned.*) She fell. I think you should look on her head.

PAMELA. Fuss, fuss, fuss.

LOUISE. (*With a faint touch of hauteur.*) Thank you, Walter. You can leave her to me, now.

WALTER. Yes, Mrs Harrington. Of course.

He gives his half bow and goes back into his own room.

LOUISE. (*Examining her daughter's head now.*) Let me see . . . . Go on upstairs. Does it hurt? (*She takes her daughter into the schoolroom.*)

PAMELA. No, it doesn't.

LOUISE. You say that as if you wanted it to. What on earth were you doing?

PAMELA. (*Exasperated.*) Nothing. I just fell. And that stupid Walter has to come in and pick me up as if I was a chandelier or something. Holding me that way.

LOUISE. (*Carefully.*) What way, darling?

PAMELA. Well, trying to carry me, as if I was a baby.

LOUISE. But he was only trying to help, wasn't he?

PAMELA. (*Angrily.*) I think he's just plain soppy.

LOUISE. Because he was worried about you?

PAMELA. Oh, Mother, for heaven's sake! You don't understand anything. . . . It's just so *undignified*, can't you see? It shows no *respect* for you. I mean, if you're two years old it's all right to pick you off floors that way, and even then it's an invasion of your privacy. If

children of two could speak, d'you know what they'd
say? 'Why can't you keep your filthy hands to yourself?'
LOUISE. I think you'd better be off on your ride before
you get into any more trouble.
PAMELA. Oh, it's one of those mornings. I bet you anything the horse breaks its leg.
They leave the schoolroom. The Symphony starts again in
WALTER'S *room.*
PAMELA. Do you think he heard?
LOUISE. Well, you weren't exactly whispering, were you?
*They go downstairs. While the stage is empty, the record
sticks. The passage is repeated several times, then the needle
is moved on.*
PAMELA. (*Coming into the living-room.*) I think I'm the
most impossible person I know. . . . But then I suppose
wonderful people always make you feel like that. Sort
of ashamed all the time.
LOUISE. He makes you feel ashamed?
PAMELA. Not exactly ashamed but, well, like in those
advertisements for washing powder. I always feel like
the grubby shirt next to the dazzling white one. He's so
fresh! Fresh and beautiful. . . . (*Brightly.*) Don't you
think he's beautiful?
LOUISE. (*Confused.*) I hadn't thought.
PAMELA. It's just what he is. He should wear a frock coat
and have consumption.
LOUISE. What nonsense.
PAMELA. Why? There *are* people like that.
LOUISE. (*With sudden irritation.*) Well, Walter certainly
isn't one of them. He's obviously quite a happy, normal
young man. There's simply no reason for you to weave
any romantic ideas about him being tragic or different
in any way.

PAMELA. (*Grandly.*) I'm afraid it's obvious you don't know him very well.

But LOUISE *is unamused. Instead, she is making an effort at self-control.*

LOUISE. If you're going, you'd better go. And I think you'd better put on a jersey.

PAMELA. Oh, phooey.

LOUISE. Darling, it's cold out.

PAMELA. It isn't really.

LOUISE. Pam, it's very cold. Now do be sensible.

PAMELA. Mother, I can't put on any more—I'd just die.

LOUISE. (*Snapping.*) Do as I say! Put on your jersey!

She leaves the room abruptly and goes up into the schoolroom. PAMELA *looks after her in surprise.*

PAMELA. (*Puzzled.*) 'Bye.

CLIVE. (*In kitchen, off.*) Pam, is that you?

PAMELA. I'm just off.

CLIVE *comes in, carrying a plate of eggs.*

CLIVE. Have a good time.

PAMELA. You should come with me.

CLIVE. I know. It does you good to get in the air.

PAMELA. (*In a wildly affected, cheerful voice.*) Well then, bye-bye, darling. You're sure there's nothing I can get you from the village? A barrel of beer? Harris tweed?

CLIVE. (*Matching her accent.*) No, thanks, old girl. Just bring back the usual papers, will you? The Hunting Gazette and the Shooting Gazette.

PAMELA. Righty-ho!

CLIVE. And the Fishing Gazette. And some wax for the old moustache.

PAMELA. Certainly, dear.

CLIVE. I say, Pamela—you are a brick!

PAMELA. (*Blowing him a kiss.*) Cheeribye, darling.

She shimmies out through the french window. CLIVE *starts eating his breakfast.* LOUISE *begins to collect the clothes which* PAMELA *has spread around the room at one time or another.* WALTER *emerges from his room. He sees* LOUISE *at work through the door, is about to go up, then thinks better of it and, instead, comes downstairs.* LOUISE *finally goes into Pamela's bedroom.*

CLIVE. Hullo.

WALTER. Hullo.

CLIVE. Do you know that a judge trying a copyright case in this country once asked learned counsel: 'What exactly *are* Brahms . . . ?'

WALTER *smiles in appreciation.*

CLIVE. What's the matter with your gramophone?

WALTER. Oh, I know; it keeps sticking. It's the table, I'm afraid, which is not quite level.

CLIVE. Oh, really? It must be one of father's. Well how are you? Clearly unwell, I should say. Only the sick and corrupt would spend a bright Sunday morning listening to music. You must know that in all decent English homes this time is reserved for sport. Staying indoors is the absolute proof of decadence.

WALTER. Yes. This is familiar to me. At home—I mean where I was born—to sit reading was an offence too.

CLIVE. You had to be out playing games?

WALTER. Games. But in small uniforms.

CLIVE. (*Scenting difficulty.*) I suppose every kid wants to be a soldier.

WALTER. Oh yes. (*Pause.*) But in England they are not told it is a good thing to be.

CLIVE. Did your uncle believe it was?

WALTER *does not reply.*

(*Cheerfully.*) Well, parents and guardians are desperately unreliable. It's what I've been telling you for weeks.

WALTER. (*Turning, smiling.*) Maybe we expect too much of them. After all, they are only us, a little older.

CLIVE. Older and more depended on.

WALTER. Exactly.

CLIVE. So not a bit like us. Absolute Power Department.

WALTER. (*Mischievously.*) Do you think *you're* going to make a very good father?

CLIVE. I don't see why not. I was a complete success as a baby. I was so demanding, I gave my parents the idea they were indispensable.

WALTER. (*Amused.*) You must have been a terrible boy.

CLIVE. Oh, desperately average, I think. Stamp collection and all.

WALTER. I wish I had known you then.

CLIVE. What on earth for?

WALTER. It would have been nice when I was a child.

CLIVE. (*Speculatively.*) Sometimes you make me wonder if you ever were.

WALTER *lowers his eyes.* CLIVE *goes on in a rush.*

Well you're such an *excluded* person. It's the thing about you.

WALTER. Not now.

CLIVE *stares at him for a moment, then speaks almost brusquely.*

CLIVE. Have you always wanted to be a teacher?

WALTER. Oh, yes. Since I was fifteen.

CLIVE. I think that's splendid. I wish *I* had something positive I wanted to be.

WALTER. Haven't you?

CLIVE. (*Gaily.*) No. I only know what I *don't* want to be. But there really isn't anything I could give a life to. The trouble is if you don't spend your life yourself, other people spend it for you. . . . As I see it, unless I suddenly feel a call from above, I'm going to wind up unemployable.

WALTER. I don't think so. Life attracts you too much. Clive, I'm sorry I ran out on you last night.

CLIVE. (*Stiffly.*) Let's forget it.

WALTER. It was kind of you to suggest a holiday together.

CLIVE *looks away.*

I know you're not happy here. . . . I would be honoured if you could talk to me. If there are things you want to say—like last night I felt there were things. Living alone is an education, you know. If you think I would be offended——

CLIVE. (*Sharply.*) I think we'll forget it! (*Pause.*) (*Indifferently.*) Walter, don't take me wrong—but are you sure you did the best thing when you left Germany?

WALTER. You think I should go back?

CLIVE. I think you ought to try.

WALTER. (*In amazement.*) You talk as if you wanted me to go away.

CLIVE. (*Very quiet.*) Yes.

WALTER. Why . . . ?

CLIVE *does not reply.*

Last night you did not want it.

CLIVE. (*With sudden desperate anger.*) Last night . . . ! I want it now. I want you to go. (*Modifying his tone with effort.*) For your sake. Only for your sake, believe me. . . . You've got a crush on our family that's almost obscene. Can't you see how lucky you are to be on your

own? Just because you never had a family you think
they're the most wonderful things in the world.

WALTER. Just because . . . !

CLIVE. Why have you got to depend all the time? It's so
damned weak!

WALTER. Clive——

CLIVE. Well, it is!

WALTER. You know nothing!

CLIVE. I can see.

WALTER. What? My parents? My father—can you see
him, in his Nazi uniform?

CLIVE. But—you told me they died.

WALTER. No. They are alive. (*Pause.*) Back in Muhlbach.
Alive. There was no uncle.

CLIVE. (*Slow.*) Your father was a Nazi?

WALTER. Oh, yes. He was a great man in the town.
People were afraid of him, and so was I. . . . When war
broke out, he went off to fight and we did not see him
for almost six years. When he came back, he was still a
Nazi. Now, everyone else was saying, 'We never liked
them. We never supported them.' But not him! 'I've
always supported them,' he said. 'Hitler was the best
man our country has seen since Bismarck. Even now we
are defeated, we are the bravest country in Europe.
Sooner or later we will win, because we have to
win. . . .' Every night he used to make me recite the old
slogans against Jews and Catholics and the Liberals.
When I forgot, he would hit me—so many mistakes,
so many hits.

CLIVE. But your mother?

WALTER. Oh, she worshipped him. Even after we found
out.

CLIVE. What?

WALTER. That during the war he—worked . . . at Auschwitz concentration camp. . . . One of the most efficient officers. Once he told me how many . . . (*He stops in distress. His voice dead with loathing.*) I could have killed him. Killed him till he was dead. And she worshipped him—my mother. She used to smile at him, stare at him—as if he owned her. And when he hit me, she would just—just look away, you know, as if what he was doing was difficult, yes—but unavoidable, like training a puppy. That was my mother.

CLIVE. (*Speaking quietly after a moment.*) And so you left?

WALTER *nods*.

I'm sorry.

WALTER. (*Recovering.*) So you see, I do know what it is to have a family. And what I look for. . . . (*In a strange tone.*) A house where now and then good spirits can sit on the roof.

CLIVE. And you think you've found it here? Do you?

WALTER *does not answer*.

You're fooling yourself every minute.

WALTER. (*Gravely.*) Don't you think I should find that out for myself?

CLIVE. Oh, for God's sake! If that horrible story was meant to change my mind, it didn't.

WALTER. I did not tell it for that.

CLIVE. Then go. Just get the hell away from here.

WALTER. Clive—my friend——

CLIVE. For my sake—*I* want it.

WALTER. But why?

CLIVE. Because . . . because I can't bear to watch.

WALTER. I don't understand you.

CLIVE. Well, then, just because. (*He turns away.*)

LOUISE *comes out of* PAMELA'S *bedroom, goes through the schoolroom and on to the landing.*

(*In private pain.*) Because. Because——

LOUISE. (*Calling downstairs.*) Walter . . . ?

WALTER *looks at* CLIVE *inquiringly, unwilling to court interruption.*

CLIVE. Go on. Answer her. It's your duty, isn't it?

WALTER. (*Low, appealing.*) Clive. . . .

CLIVE. (*Turning on him ferociously.*) Answer her!

As WALTER *stands irresolutely,* CLIVE *turns again and goes out abruptly, half running, through the french window.* LOUISE *descends the stairs.*

LOUISE. (*Calling.*) Walter!

WALTER. (*Faintly, looking after* CLIVE.) I'm in here, Mrs Harrington.

LOUISE. (*Coming into the living-room.*) Ah, there you are. My dear boy, all alone . . . ? (*Going to sofa.*) Come and talk to me, it's not good for you to be on your own too much.

WALTER. I was not alone. Clive was here. He's just gone out.

LOUISE. Out?—Where?

WALTER. I don't know . . . . Mrs Harrington, I am worried for him.

LOUISE. (*Smiling.*) Poor Hibou, you worry about everybody, don't you? But you mustn't about Clive, really. It's just a tiny case of old-fashioned jealousy, that's all. Well, it's only to be expected, isn't it? We've always been so wonderfully close, he and I.

WALTER. (*Courteously.*) Of course.

LOUISE. It's nothing serious. One day he'll understand about women. At the moment, of course, he thinks there must only be room in my heart for one boy. So silly. . . .

(*Warmly.*) I don't believe you can ration friendship, do you?

WALTER. (*Admiringly.*) With someone like you it is not possible.

LOUISE. Nor with you, my dear. You know, last night held the most beautiful moments I've known for many years. I felt—well, that you and I could have a really warm friendship. Even with the difference . . . I mean in—in our ages.

WALTER. Between friends there are no ages, I think.

LOUISE. (*Tenderly.*) I like to think that, too.

WALTER. Oh, it's true. Like in a family—you never think how old people are, because you keep growing together.

LOUISE. Yes. Dear little owl. . . . What's the matter . . . ? Are you embarrassed?

He shakes his head 'No'.

It's the last thing you must ever be with me.

WALTER *smiles.*

What are you thinking? Come on: tell me.

WALTER. Some things grow more when they are not talked about.

LOUISE. Try, anyway. I want you to.

WALTER. (*Looking away from her.*) It is only that you have made me wonder——

LOUISE. (*Prompting eagerly.*) Tell me.

WALTER. (*Lowering his voice still more.*) Mrs Harrington, forgive me for asking this, but do you think it's possible for someone to find a new mother?

LOUISE *sits very still. The expression of eagerness fades, and its remnant hardens on her face. She stares at him.*

Have I offended you?

LOUISE. (*Smiles, without joy.*) Of course not. I am . . . very touched.

WALTER. (*Moved.*) Thank you. (*Eagerly.*) That is why I feel I can talk to you about Clive, for example. I am most worried for him. He is not happy now. And I do not think it is jealousy. It is something else—more deep in him—trying to explode. Like the beginning of an earthquake or so.

LOUISE *rises.*

LOUISE. (*With increasing coolness.*) Really, my dear, don't you think you're being a little over-dramatic?

WALTER. (*Dogged.*) No. I mean exactly this. It is hard to explain.

LOUISE. (*Wryly.*) I appreciate your attempt. . . . But really, I'm sure I know my children a little better than you.

WALTER. (*Persisting.*) Of course. But just in this case— with Clive—I feel something which frightens me—I don't know why——

LOUISE. (*Her temper breaking.*) Oh, for heaven's sake!

WALTER *recoils.*

(*Recovering quickly.*) I mean. . . . After all, as you admit yourself, you *are* only a new-comer to the family, remember. (*Sweetly.*) Now why don't you go and play me some of your nice music?

WALTER *looks confused and lowers his eyes before her strained smile. He goes into the kitchen.* LOUISE *is left alone.*

CURTAIN

ACT TWO

SCENE TWO

The same night, after supper.

The living-room is empty. Up in the schoolroom, WALTER
is hearing PAMELA *in her irregular verbs. They are sitting
in their usual position at the table.*

PAMELA. Je meurs, tu meurs, il meurt, nous meurons——
WALTER. No.
PAMELA. It must be.
WALTER. *Mou*——
PAMELA. Mourons. Oh, phooey. . . . You know, this is the
perfect way to end today. It's been a stinker, hasn't it?
WALTER. Has it? I thought you had a good ride this
morning.
PAMELA. Oh, that . . . I mean the atmosphere since I got
back. What Mother calls the *aura*. And Clive not coming
in for lunch or dinner. D'you think he's run away?
WALTER. I think we do more French.
PAMELA. Mother was livid tonight when he didn't turn
up. That's funny, too. I'd have thought Daddy would
have been the one to explode, but he didn't say a word. . . .
Do you think Clive's lost his memory or something?
WALTER. What is the future of 'mourir'?
PAMELA. Perhaps he's been kidnapped. Just think of
Daddy paying ransom. I wonder if he would.
WALTER. I think Clive can take care of himself. Now,
please, Pamela——

PAMELA. Oh, I'm sick of French! It's Sunday, and that's supposed to be a Day of Rest.

WALTER. Yesterday you said you felt Jewish and Saturday was your day of rest.

PAMELA. That was Saturday—not Sunday. Today I'm going to have a hot bath and go straight to bed and read. Mary gave me a most important scientific book last week and I just haven't had a moment to glance at it.

WALTER. (*Suspiciously.*) What kind of science?

PAMELA. Actually it's a kind of story.

WALTER. (*Resigned.*) Ah-ha.

PAMELA. But completely scientific. It tells what would happen if the earth got invaded by Venus. The people are just sweeties. They're all ten foot high and covered with blue jelly.

WALTER. Very educational.

LOUISE *comes out of her bedroom. She looks strained and anxious.*

LOUISE. Pamela——

PAMELA. There you are. You can't even have a scientific discussion any more without being interrupted by the world of triviality.

LOUISE *comes into the schoolroom.* WALTER *rises.*

LOUISE. (*To her daughter.*) How's the bruise, darling? I've turned on your bath.

PAMELA. Has Clive come back yet?

LOUISE. (*Wearily, but with a vestige of deep anger.*) No. Not yet. . . . (*Softening.*) Now get into your bath and don't dawdle, will you?

She goes to the door. Having virtually ignored WALTER, *who has stood uncomfortably by the table, she just notices him on the way out.*

Good night, Walter.

WALTER. Good night, Mrs Harrington.

LOUISE *goes downstairs.*

PAMELA. (*Whispering.*) She looks as if she needs a fizzy.

WALTER. Ssh! Tch. Tch.

PAMELA. Well, she does. Mother always goes like that when she's lost an argument. It's meant to mean she's been misunderstood.

WALTER. She is worried about Clive.

PAMELA. Phooey! Anyone would think he was still a baby, the way she goes on. (*Wickedly.*) I hope he stays out all night. Wouldn't it be wonderful if he was giving babies to all the schoolgirls in Ipswich . . . ? (*She goes into her room, where she calls in her affected voice.*) Well, I'd better go and have my bath, dear boy. Oh Lord, Sunday night. Breakfast at half past seven for that rotten train. I think Mondays stink. . . .

She returns with her nightdress and dressing-gown.

Is there any religion with its Day of Rest on Mondays?

WALTER. Yes. The religion of Lazy Girls.

PAMELA. Oh, you are brutish!

She goes off for her bath. Presently the front door opens. STANLEY *comes in and walks into the living-room, taking off his overcoat.*

LOUISE. (*Hearing the noise of his entry.*) Clive? Oh, it's you. . . .

STANLEY. (*Coming in.*) Isn't he back?

LOUISE. No.

STANLEY. Well, no one's seen him in the village. He hasn't been in any of the pubs.

LOUISE. (*Bitterly.*) The pubs. Always the pubs.

STANLEY. Well, where else would he be likely to go? You know what the trouble is? Your son's turning into a drunkard.

LOUISE. The way you've been behaving lately's enough to make anyone drink. No one would think he's your son. You treat him abominably.

STANLEY. Do I?

LOUISE. You haven't the faintest idea how to deal with sensitive people. If I was Clive, I'd have run away from home long ago.

STANLEY. (*Bitterly.*) If it weren't for the saving grace of his mother. His sensitive mother.

LOUISE. At least I understand him. I make an effort. Just because you can't see beyond the end of your selfish, commonplace nose——

STANLEY. (*Savage.*) Shut up!

LOUISE. Charming.

STANLEY. (*His pain also becoming rage.*) And what have you done for him that's so wonderful, may I ask? I'll tell you. Turned him into a snivelling little neurotic. A mother's boy. That's what!

LOUISE. (*Trying to recover poise.*) That's not true.

STANLEY. And I'll tell you something else. He's going peculiar. Yes: loony, if you want to know. He talked to me last night and I didn't understand one word he said.

LOUISE. (*Loftily.*) That doesn't surprise me.

STANLEY. It was like listening to a lunatic.

LOUISE. And that's my fault too? Just because I take an interest in our son, which you've never bothered to do in all these years, I'm driving him insane.

STANLEY. (*With wild demand in his tone.*) And when I tried to take an interest, what happened? When I offered to teach him things——

LOUISE. What things?

STANLEY. Golf—swimming—I don't know, I can't re-member. Who was it said, 'Clive's too delicate'? 'Clive can't waste his time on silly games. He's got his reading to do. . . .'

LOUISE. So it was wrong of me to encourage his reading?

STANLEY. He was my son as much as yours!

LOUISE. Yes, and what did you want to do for him? Push him straight into your third-rate furniture business for the rest of his life. Well, that's not good enough for *me*, Stanley.

STANLEY. (*Cutting through this.*) Well, he was my son, wasn't he?

LOUISE. He still *is*, my dear.

STANLEY. (*Hard.*) No. Not any more. You've seen to that.

LOUISE *looks away from him sharply.*

LOUISE. (*Collected.*) That's the nastiest thing you've ever said to me.

STANLEY. I didn't mean it.

LOUISE. Yes, you did.

STANLEY. (*Wearily.*) I don't know what I mean any more. . . . It's all so bloody mixed up.

LOUISE. Must you swear?

STANLEY. *I* don't know. . . .

LOUISE. I can't stand much more. I just can't.

STANLEY. (*Dead.*) What?

LOUISE. It's no good, Stanley. My life was never meant to be like this—limited this way . . . I know I'm un-predictable sometimes. I say things I don't mean. But don't you see I'm just so frustrated I don't know what I'm doing half the time? I'm sorry, but it's the only word, Stanley. There are times I feel I'm being abso-lutely choked to death—suffocated under piles of English blankets. Yes, my dear: I'm not English and won't ever be, no matter how hard I try. Can't you ever under-stand that you married someone who's really a Parisian at heart? A Frenchwoman, my dear man, with all that means—faults too, of course—frivolity and being irresponsible. If I've disappointed you, it's because I've never really become *acclimatée*—you know, acclimatized —that's all. I've never been able to take your world of shops and business seriously. Can't you understand?

He makes a futile gesture.

STANLEY. (*Flat.*) What do you want me to do, Louise? Louise, I'm asking you. D'you want a divorce . . . ? Well?

LOUISE. Oh, it's all so vulgar.

STANLEY. (*Tired.*) I'm a vulgar man.

LOUISE. Do *you*? What do *you* want?

STANLEY. (*Plainly.*) I'm too old to start again.

LOUISE. That's a nice way of putting it.

STANLEY. Oh, for heaven's sake, *nice* . . . And there's Pam. It wouldn't do her any good.

LOUISE. I notice you don't mention Clive.

STANLEY. Clive's no longer a child. Although it probably upsets you to think of it, he's almost twenty years old.

LOUISE. I think it's you who haven't gathered that.

STANLEY. Don't start—just don't start.

LOUISE. I didn't begin it.

STANLEY. (*Getting up, frantic.*) Louise . . . ! (*After a moment, in an altered voice—not looking at her.*) Do you think if we went away it would help? Just the two of us, alone together? We could go back to Monte.

PAMELA *comes from the bathroom in her dressing-gown, and goes downstairs.*

LOUISE. You know I can't stand the place.

STANLEY. (*Controlling himself.*) Well, anywhere. . . .

PAMELA *enters.*

LOUISE. Clive?—Oh, it's you, Pam,

PAMELA. Yes mother. Isn't Clive back yet?

LOUISE. Don't worry, darling. He'll be in soon. Now sleep well, and don't read too late.

PAMELA. Good night. Good night Daddy. (*She kisses him and goes out and upstairs to the schoolroom.*)

STANLEY. It's worth a try, isn't it, Louise?

LOUISE. Yes, Stanley. It's worth a try.

PAMELA. (*In the schoolroom.*) Good night.

WALTER. (*In the schoolroom.*) Sleep tight.

PAMELA. Mind the bugs don't bite.

PAMELA *goes into her room and shuts the door.* LOUISE *pauses for a moment. When she speaks her tone is light, almost winning and subservient: wholly without a sense of calculation.*

LOUISE. Stanley, I want to ask you to do something for me—something rather difficult.

STANLEY. What's that?

LOUISE. It's to do with Pamela. I feel it's something you can manage better than I can.

STANLEY. Pam?

LOUISE. Actually, it's about Walter. I'm afraid he's having rather a bad effect on her. She's just at that stage, you know—impressionable, romantic—long walks in the moonlight. Well, I'm afraid she's got a bit of a crush. Nothing serious of course—she'll soon get over it. But —well, it's her first and, naturally, she's rather unhappy. She threw quite a little scene this morning, as a matter of fact . . . The boy, of course, is a Continental, and can't resist angling for admiration all the time. So he flatters her, I suppose, and pays her compliments. In the normal way I'd encourage it: it would help to give her a little poise. But in this case she seems to be taking it all just a little too seriously.

STANLEY. You want me to talk to her?

LOUISE. No. Something rather more drastic I'm afraid. I think we must let Walter go. In the most tactful way, of course. Actually I think the sooner the better.

STANLEY. I see.

LOUISE. I think he's up in the schoolroom now—shall I ask him to come down? I'll make myself scarce. And you will be tactful, won't you?

CLIVE *blunders in through the front door. He is drunk but— as on the previous evening—perfectly coherent.*
Clive!

CLIVE. Good evening, all.

STANLEY. Would you mind telling me where you've been? Did you hear me? You've been out since twelve.

CLIVE. Like the tide. But we're back, you see.

STANLEY. Answer me!

CLIVE. Why the hell do we always have to ask expected questions?

STANLEY. Now listen my boy, you've been drink——

LOUISE. (*Quietly.*) Why don't you go upstairs, dear, and do what I asked you to?

STANLEY. (*To* LOUISE.) Very well. I'll leave you to look after your sensitive son.

He goes out of the room and up the stairs. At the top, he knocks at WALTER'S *door, receives no answer, and, less resolutely, approaches the schoolroom.*

LOUISE. (*Bitterly.*) Your father and I have been worried to death.

CLIVE. (*Insolently.*) Do I detect a new note in the air? Your father and I? How splendid. The birth of a new moral being. Your-father-and-I . . . When did you last see your father-and-I? Or is it just a new alliance . . . ?

All the same, I congratulate you. I always thought you two ought to get married.

LOUISE. You're drunk and disgusting. I'll get you something to eat and you can go up to bed.

CLIVE. (*Coldly.*) Your-father-and-I will now get your supper.

LOUISE *goes into the kitchen. The brightness of the room troubles* CLIVE. *He shuffles clumsily across and turns off the lights so that only the glow from the fire remains as he sinks wearily into the armchair and covers his eyes.*

STANLEY *enters the schoolroom.*

STANLEY. Are you busy?

WALTER. (*Standing up; as always, made nervous by his appearance.*) Of course not, Mr Harrington. I was just reading—is Clive back yet?

STANLEY. He just came in—drunk. Do you drink? I don't remember seeing you.

WALTER. Not very much, no.

STANLEY. Sensible. (*Pause.*) My son drinks. A lot. Doesn't he? (WALTER *says nothing.*) Why does he drink? Can you see any good reason for it?

WALTER. I do not think people drink for good reasons.

STANLEY. Sit down.

WALTER *sits wearily.* STANLEY *sits also, facing him at the table.*

You don't think much of me, do you?

WALTER. Mr Harrington——

STANLEY. Why? Because I'm not educated. Is that it?

WALTER. Of course not.

STANLEY. Then why? Because the children say things?

WALTER. Mr Harrington, please, I——

STANLEY. And what do they know? People say parents are selfish. They've got nothing on children. Do children ever think about anything but themselves? *Their* troubles... ? As if nobody ever had 'em before. Well, ...? You ought to know. You teach 'em.

WALTER. (*Softly.*) I think children are not so able to help themselves with their troubles.

STANLEY. (*Not really listening.*) I tell you, children are the most selfish things in the world. . . . So he drinks. Did you know it was my fault? I drive him to it. So I hear.

WALTER *says nothing*.

Well . . . ? Have you lost your tongue?

WALTER. (*Very low.*) No.

STANLEY. I'll tell you why he drinks. So he can get over being with me. Have you noticed how this family of mine never get together in this house? Are you afraid of me?

WALTER. (*Straight.*) No.

STANLEY. Well, that's a wonder. My son is. That's something else I hear. What do you think?

WALTER. I think . . . yes.

STANLEY. (*Blankly.*) Do you?

WALTER. (*With difficulty.*) I think he feels you do not love him, but still are expecting him to love you.

STANLEY. Rubbish.

WALTER. (*Retreating at once.*) I'm sorry. You did ask me.

STANLEY. He's my *son*. How can he think that?

WALTER. He does not wish to be alone with you because always he feels you are—well—judging him. When you look at him, he sees you are thinking—'How useless he is'.

STANLEY. And when he looks at me—what's *he* thinking? Ah, that's a different story, isn't it? (*Bitterly.*) 'How common.'

WALTER. Oh, no——

STANLEY. Don't tell me. Common! I've seen it too often.

WALTER. (*Overbearing him urgently.*) No! You are wrong about him. You see in front of you he must always justify his life. His Greek, maybe, or because he loves an opera. When a boy must apologize for ears and eyes, it is very bad.

STANLEY. Apologize? When have I asked him to apologize?

WALTER. That's not what I mean.

STANLEY. Then why use such ridiculous words? I can see now where he gets them from.

WALTER. (*Gravely.*) Your son has got nothing from me. I wish he had. Sir, your son needs help. Will he get it?

STANLEY. He can always come to me. He knows that.

WALTER. (*Raising his voice slightly*) And will he come? *Does* he come?

STANLEY. (*Gathering dignity about him.*) As a matter of fact, we had a very frank talk last night. You didn't know that, did you? What are you thinking?

WALTER. You know, you are very like your son, Mr Harrington.

STANLEY. (*Sarcastic.*) Oh, yes. In education, I suppose.

WALTER. I say too much always. . . .

STANLEY *shrugs. Suddenly he begins to talk more or less to himself.*

STANLEY. What's it matter? . . . You start a family, work and plan. Suddenly you turn round and there's nothing there. Probably never was. What's a family, anyway? Just—just kids with your blood in 'em. There's no reason why they should like you. . . . You go on expecting it, of course, but it's silly really. Like expecting 'em to know what they meant to you when they were babies.

They're not supposed to know, perhaps. It's not natural, really, when you come to think of it. You can't expect anybody to know what they mean to somebody else—it's not the way of things. (*He stops, confused. When he resumes, his voice is even softer.*) There's just nothing. Bloody nothing.

Unseen by him, WALTER *gestures towards him in a futile attempt at communication. He goes on staring into space, not heeding the tutor at all.*

You get a wife and family and you work for them. And all the time you think: it'll be better next year. Next year it'll be all right. The children going to prep school, leaving it. Short trousers, long trousers. Perhaps he'll make the rugger fifteen or the cricket team or something—anything—and then his first girl friend and taking her home—or perhaps just keeping her to himself till he's sure. . . . (*Frankly.*) But nothing . . . . Nothing . . . And now he hates me.

WALTER. No. . . .

STANLEY. (*Focusing again.*) D'you think I don't know? How sensitive do you have to be for that? Tell me— because I don't know too much about that sort of thing. (*His bitterness rises once more*) I'm always too busy making money. (*Violently.*) Go on, tell me. Sensitive people have deep feelings, don't they? They suffer a lot!

WALTER. Please Mr Harrington——

STANLEY. (*Violently.*) I don't want to hear!

WALTER. Excuse me, sir.

Pause.

Moved and bewildered, WALTER *rises and then leaves the room. On the landing he hesitates for a moment then, on an impulse, goes downstairs.* STANLEY *is left staring into space. He rises and moves aimlessly to the window. He stares out of it unseeingly, then sits slowly in the chair vacated by* WALTER, *so that we see only his back.*

WALTER *reaches the living-room, where* CLIVE *has been lying inert in the armchair, in a strange awkward position suggesting acute depression.*

WALTER. Clive? What's the matter? Why are you sitting in the dark? I've been talking to your father. He thinks you hate him.

CLIVE *does not appear to hear.*

Clive, listen to me. . . . The Kings of Egypt were gods. Everything they did was right, everything they said was true, and when they died, they grew faces of gold. You must try to forgive your parents for being average and wrong when you worshipped them once. Why are you so afraid? Is it—because you have no girl friend? Oh, you are so silly. Silly. Do you think sex will change you? Put you into a different world, where everything will mean more to you? I thought so too, once. I thought it would change me into a man so my father could never touch me again. I didn't know exactly what it would be like, but I thought it would burn me and bring me terrible pain. But afterwards, I'd be strong and very wise. . . . There was a girl in Muhlbach. She worked in her mother's grocery shop. One night I had a few drinks and, just for a joke, I broke into her bedroom through the window. I stayed with her all night. And I entered heaven. I really did. Between her arms was the only place in the world that mattered. When daylight came, I felt I had changed for ever. A little later I got up. I looked round, but the room was exactly the same. This was incomprehensible. It should have been so huge now—filled with air. But it seemed very small and stuffy, and outside it was raining. I remember I hated the soap for lying there in the dish just as it had done the night before. I watched her putting on her clothes. I thought: 'We're tied together now by an invisible thread.' And then she said, 'It's nine o'clock: I must be off'—and went downstairs to open the shop. Then, I looked into the mirror: at least my eyes would be different. (*Ironically.*) They were a little red, yes—but I was exactly the same—still a boy. Rain was still here. And all the problems of yesterday were still waiting.

He pauses and puts his hand on CLIVE'S *arm.*

Sex by itself is nothing, believe me. Just like breathing —only important when it goes wrong. And Clive, this only happens if you're afraid of it. What are you thinking . . . ? Please talk to me.

CLIVE. (*Very low.*) Walter. . . .

WALTER. Yes?

CLIVE. (*Low, his head buried.*) What's wrong with me?

WALTER. There's nothing wrong with you. Nothing.

CLIVE. Don't fool me. I know.

WALTER. There's nothing wrong but in your mind. What you think about.

CLIVE. (*Despairing.*) What is it? What have they done to me?

WALTER. Clive——Your parents love you. Everything they have done has been from love. I am sure of this.

CLIVE. Then God save me from love.

WALTER. He will not. . . . You have more in you than any man I've ever met.

CLIVE. (*Breaking free.*) Stop it. . . .

WALTER. Clive, my dear friend, let me help you.

CLIVE. Cut that out!

WALTER. What?

CLIVE. Pity. D'you think I'd have let him take the guts out of me, if his attempts to love me weren't so rotten to watch?

WALTER. (*Gently.*) I don't pity you, Clive. And you mustn't pity yourself. You can end this and you must. You must leave here. You—not me. At the moment you are—(*gestures*)—on your family. I don't know the word. Like a butterfly on a pin.

CLIVE. (*With distaste.*) Impaled.

WALTER. Yes. And you must get off the pin. At the end of term in Cambridge, don't come back here. Go anywhere else you like. Join your American friend singing. Go into a factory. Anything. The important thing is this—as soon as you are out of here, people will start telling you who you are. (*Tenderly.*) Maybe you will not like it, but that's nonsense, you must always like the truth.

CLIVE *shakes his head 'No'.*

You think you can't do this, but you must. Oh, is this so difficult? . . . I could tell you what *I* want.

CLIVE. Go on.

WALTER. To live in England. To be happy teaching. One day to marry. To have children, and many English friends . . . And now you. What do *you* want?

Pause.

CLIVE. (*Faintly.*) Something—I'm not sure. (*Intimately.*) Yes—I think I want . . . to achieve something that only I could do. I want to fall in love with just one person. To know what it is to bless and be blessed. And to serve a great cause with devotion. (*Appealing.*) I want to be *involved*.

WALTER. Then break the glass! Get out of the coffin!

Jump up and begin yourself. Make up your own time without one minute when you don't care who you are.

STANLEY *rises from the table in the schoolroom and leaves the room. He goes downstairs.*

Trust everything, not because it's wise, but because not to trust will kill you. Trust me, for instance. I'll see you often. But you must go away from here. Say yes—you will go.

STANLEY *enters the room, unheard.*

CLIVE. (*Nodding.*) Yes. I'll go.

WALTER. The next vacation.

CLIVE. The next vacation.

WALTER. Good!

CLIVE. Isn't it silly? We seem to spend all the time ordering each other out of the house!

WALTER. A very friendly way to spend the time.

The main light snaps on. STANLEY *stands in the doorway.*

STANLEY. Clive—don't you think it's time you went to bed?

CLIVE. I suppose so.

WALTER. (*Gently to* CLIVE.) You're sure you are all right now?

CLIVE. Yes, I'm all right.

CLIVE *goes out, upstairs, and into his room.* WALTER *gives his half-bow and makes as if to follow, but is stopped by* STANLEY.

STANLEY. (*Raging.*) Just who the hell do you think you are?

WALTER. I'm sorry?

STANLEY. The world owes you a living: that's it.

WALTER. Mr Harrington——

STANLEY. (*Brutally.*) Don't 'Mr Harrington' me, with your smarmy voice and bowing from the waist. You

had the gall to patronize me just now—tell me what's
wrong with my home. . . .

WALTER. You forget—you asked me for my opinion.

STANLEY. Oh, yes. And what else did I ask you to do?
Turn my son into a cissy?

WALTER. Your son is a fine, intelligent boy.

STANLEY. He's a mess, that's what he is. And it's your
fault.

WALTER. My fault——?

STANLEY. (*Blindly.*) Yes, yours. *Yours.* You, the arty
boys. It's you who've taken him. . . . (*Hurling the names
as if they were insults.*) Shakespeare! Beethoven !. . . All
the time, till I can't touch him . . . . What gave you the
right to steal my boy?

WALTER. (*With pity.*) You will believe what you
please.

STANLEY. I'm not blind you know—and I'm not deaf. I
heard you telling him just now—'Get out of this house'
you said.

WALTER. Yes, I did.

STANLEY. How dare you say a thing like that? What
right have you—in my house, working for me—to say
a thing like that?

WALTER. My friendship for your son.

STANLEY. Oh, of course! And your friendship with my
daughter Pamela too, what about that?

WALTER. Pamela?

STANLEY. (*Crisply, with satisfaction.*) Your employer,
Mrs Harrington, has asked me to dismiss you because
she thinks you are having a bad effect upon our
daughter.

Slight pause.

WALTER. (*Incredulous.*) Mrs Harrington said this?

STANLEY. Yes.

WALTER. But it's not true. Not true at all. . . .

STANLEY. (*Carefully.*) No. I don't think it is.

Slight pause. WALTER *looks in utter distress and bewilderment at* STANLEY.

WALTER. Then—why . . . ?

STANLEY. Could it be because you've been trying to make love to my wife?

WALTER *reacts sharply to protest.* STANLEY *goes on in the same quiet tone.*

You filthy German bastard.

The boy winces as if he has been slapped.

Once a German, always a German. Take what you want and the hell with everyone else.

WALTER *stands rigid, with face averted.* STANLEY *moves round him as if he were a statue.*

You're a fool, too. Did you really think my wife would ever risk anything for you? Oh, I know it's very cultured to look down on money, but that's a very different thing from giving it up. Well, now you've had your chips, and she's sent me to give them to you.

A long pause.

When WALTER *speaks, it is very quietly, from the depth of his humiliation.*

WALTER. You really believe . . . ? It's not possible. . . .

STANLEY. Oh, yes—it's quite possible. I've got a perfect witness, 'unimpeachable' as we say in England.

WALTER *looks at him.*

Can't you guess . . . ? No . . . ? (*Hard.*) Your pal. Your good pal.

WALTER. (*Whispering.*) Clive?

STANLEY. Of course Clive: who else?

WALTER. (*In disbelief.*) No!

STANLEY. He told me he saw you both—in this room, last night.

WALTER. No—oh, no—but——

STANLEY. Do you know what we do with people like you in England? Chuck 'em out. (*Lowering his voice.*) I'm going to fix it so you never get your naturalization papers. I m going to write to the immigration people. I'll write tonight, and tell them all about you. I'll say—let's see—'Much though I hate to complain about people behind their backs, I feel it my duty in this case to warn you about this young German's standard of morality. Whilst under my roof, he attempted to force his attentions on my young daughter, who is only fourteen.' Try and get your papers after that. They'll send you back to the place where you belong! . . .

LOUISE *enters from kitchen.* WALTER *faces away from them.*

LOUISE. Stanley, I thought you were upstairs——Walter! What's the matter?

STANLEY. I did what you asked me.

LOUISE. Yes, but *how* did you do it? I can just imagine.

She puts down the tray and goes to WALTER.

Was he very brutal, mon cher? Oh . . . poor little Hibou——

WALTER *does not look at her.*

But you know yourself it's for the best, don't you? It's so silly, being . . . upset. . . .

Suddenly, unexpectedly, WALTER *falls on his knees and grasps her hand in an imploring, desperate, filial gesture.*

WALTER. Don't . . . I beg of you. . . .

STANLEY *moves sharply away from them.*

LOUISE. (*Trying to free herself.*) Walter, please. . . .

WALTER. No. . . .

LOUISE. Really, Walter . . . ! Get up at once.

WALTER. Please . . . don't. . . .

LOUISE. Do you hear me?

STANLEY. (*Who has turned round.*) Too sensitive for you, my dear?

LOUISE. (*Stung by his mockery.*) Walter! Will you stop making an exhibition of yourself? You're being embarrassing and ridiculous.

He stiffens. She moderates her tone.

Now, please get up, and stop making an exhibition of yourself.

He does so, slowly relinquishing her hand and looking away from her.

I'm sorry, but I'm afraid you deserved to be spoken to like that. I'm really very disappointed in you. . . . Both our children have been considerably disturbed by your presence in our house. And of course I could never allow that. They have always come first with me. I'm sure you understand.

No reply.

Now, as regards finances, we will make it as easy for you as possible. You could manage a month's wages, I think, Stanley?

STANLEY. Oh . . . yes.

LOUISE. There you are. A month's wage. I call that quite generous, don't you?

WALTER. (*In a remote, disinterested voice.*) Yes.

LOUISE. Good. (*Seeing his distress.*) Oh, don't look so stricken, Hibou. It makes it so much more difficult for everybody.

A pause. WALTER *leaves the room.*

(*Calling after him.*) Well, of all the embarrassing,

hysterical scenes...! (*Rounding on* STANLEY.) You seem to have handled it brilliantly.

As WALTER *reaches the landing,* CLIVE *appears.*

CLIVE. Walter——

WALTER. No!

WALTER *shakes him off and rushes into his room, slamming the door.*

CLIVE *enters from hall.*

CLIVE. What's the matter with Walter?

LOUISE. He's a little upset. There's some supper here for you—you'd better eat it.

CLIVE. Why is he upset? What's been going on down here?

LOUISE. I think it's better if we don't talk about it.

CLIVE. Do you want to talk about it, Father? (STANLEY *is standing at the window curtain. He is trembling.*) Father—I'm asking you a question. Do you hear me?

LOUISE. Don't be so impertinent, Clive—speaking to your father like that.

CLIVE. Ah—your father and I—the new alliance. What have you both done to Walter—both of you? I'm only asking a simple question.

A pause. STANLEY *turns then, with difficulty. He speaks.*

STANLEY. If you really want to know, I told him what you said last night about him and your mother.

LOUISE. Me?

STANLEY. Yes, my dear. You and your daughter's tutor —a pretty picture.

LOUISE. (*Shaken.*) What did he tell you? Clive, what did you say?

STANLEY. Never mind—I didn't believe it.

LOUISE. I want to know what Clive said to you.

STANLEY. What's it matter——It never matters what he says.

CLIVE. So you didn't believe me?

STANLEY. Did you really think I would?

CLIVE. Then why did you talk to Walter just now as if you did? Why was he so upset?—Well?

But STANLEY *is past reply, past justification or even the attitude of parenthood. He opens his mouth to speak, stares at them both in mute pain, then goes out without a word, and upstairs to his room.* CLIVE *stares after him.*

CLIVE. Well, Mother?

LOUISE. Jou-jou! Jou-jou, you didn't suggest . . . . But this is horrible. . . . You couldn't have said such things about me, surely?

CLIVE. Yes—I said them.

LOUISE. But why?

CLIVE. I don't know.

LOUISE. Jou-jou!

CLIVE. I don't know. I do something terrible that I'll remember all my life, that'll make me sick whenever I think of it—and I don't know why.

LOUISE. You're ill—you must be.

CLIVE. Oh no! It only means *I* can damage people too— that's all. I can dish it out—just like everyone else.

LOUISE. But it's not true. It's not true, what you said.

CLIVE. True? I told the lie, yes. But what I felt *under* the lie—about you and Walter—was that so untrue? No, don't answer, because whatever you said just wouldn't be real. You've forgotten what it is to be honest about true feelings. True! The only true thing I know is what's happened to him—my father!

LOUISE. You're ill.

CLIVE. Yes—and you're so worried about me. Department of Flattering Unction.

LOUISE. Clive—you frighten me. Why are you being so terrible? What have I done?

CLIVE. Don't you know? Can't you *see* what you've done? There isn't a Stanley Harrington any more. We've broken him in bits between us.

LOUISE. I don't know what you're talking about. I really don't.

CLIVE. No—you don't. . . . Poor man.

LOUISE. Clive—you hate me.

CLIVE. I hate. Isn't that enough? (*Pause.*) Is the war in this house never going to end?

LOUISE. War?

CLIVE. The war you both declared when you married. The culture war with me as ammunition. 'Let's show him how small he is'—'Let's show her where she gets off'. *And always through me!* . . . He wasn't always a bully —I'm sure of that. You made him into one.

LOUISE. I'll not go on with this conversation another moment. It's obscene. Your father's upset. Simply upset, that's all.

CLIVE. But why is he upset?

LOUISE. About something I asked him to do.

CLIVE. It was something to do with Walter wasn't it? What have you done to Walter?

LOUISE. If you must know—he's been dismissed.

CLIVE. Mother—no!

LOUISE. I assure you there were excellent reasons.

CLIVE. But you can't dismiss him. You *can't*. Not even you—— (*In sudden despair.*) He can't go away from here!

She looks at him curiously.

LOUISE. (*Calmly.*) If you want to know, I did it for Pam.

I'm afraid his influence over her was getting rather stronger than I cared for.

A slight pause. She sits.

CLIVE. (*Also calm.*) I see.

The slow third movement of Mahler's Fourth Symphony is heard from WALTER'S *room.*

LOUISE. Well, evidently the boy himself is not so shattered by the news as you are. . . . Don't you think you'd better eat your supper?

CLIVE. (*Matter of fact.*) What was it? Jealousy? Shame, when you saw them so innocent together? Or just the sheer vulgarity of competing with one's own daughter?

LOUISE. How dare you!

CLIVE. Dearest Mother, who are you trying to fool? I know your rules. Don't give sympathy to a man if others are giving it too—he'll never see how unique you are. Besides, doing what everyone else does is just too vulgar. Like going to Monte, or falling in love.

LOUISE *bursts into tears.*

(*Anguished.*) Mother!

She sobs helplessly for a moment.

(*With a wild, hopeless grief.*) Oh, it goes on and on. No meeting. . . . Never. . . . Why can't we be important to each other? Why can't we ever come back into the room and be new to each other? Why doesn't a night's sleep lying all those dark hours with ourselves forgotten and then coming alive again, why doesn't it ever change us? Give us new things to see—new things to say too: not just 'Eat your eggs', or 'You were in late'—the old dreariness. (*Desperately, to his mother.*) I want to *know* you. But you wonderful—changed into yourself. . . . Don't you understand? So that you can change me.

She sits unmoving, no longer crying, giving no indication of having heard. Her son kneels to her and embraces her with desperate tenderness.

(*Tenderly.*) Maman . . . Maman, chérie . . .

For a moment she endures it, then, with a gesture of repulsion, she shakes him off.

LOUISE. Don't——!

CLIVE. (*Falling back.*) Maman . . .

LOUISE. (*Rounding on him.*) D'you think you're the only one can ask terrible questions? Supposing I ask a few. Supposing I ask them . . . ! You ought to be glad Walter's going, but you're not. Why not? Why aren't you glad? You want him to stay, don't you? You want him to stay very much. Why?

CLIVE. (*In panic.*) Maman!

LOUISE. (*Pitiless.*) Why . . . ? You said filthy things to your father about me. Filth and lies. Why? Can you think of an answer? . . . Why, Clive? Why about me and Walter? Why? Why . . . ? Why?

CLIVE. (*In a scream.*) You're *killing* . . . !

She stops, her arm stretched out in a sudden gesture of true maternal protectiveness. CLIVE *has both his hands before his face, as if to ward off a blow. In the silence, they both become aware of a strange sound: the record playing in* WALTER'S *room has stuck. The same phrase is being played again and again. The needle is not moved on. The pause is held.* CLIVE *lowers his hands. A dawning alarm expresses itself on* LOUISE'S *face.*

STANLEY *comes from his room and appears on the landing, drawn by the noise. He goes to* WALTER'S *room and knocks. There is no reply. He turns the handle, but has to push the door hard to get it open.* WALTER'S *jacket is stuffed under it. He disappears for a second, then comes out coughing.*

STANLEY. Louise!

LOUISE. Stanley?

She runs upstairs. CLIVE *still stays where he is.*

STANLEY. (*Returning to the room.*) Get the doctor.

LOUISE *arrives on the landing. The record is switched off.*

LOUISE. What is it? What's happened?

STANLEY. (*From the bedroom.*) It's Walter . . . get a doctor . . . Quick.

LOUISE *runs downstairs again, coughing from the gas.* CLIVE *has moved slowly out of the room and starts going upstairs as his mother comes down them and starts to telephone.*

LOUISE. Hello . . . Hello . . . 342, please.

STANLEY *re-emerges, dragging the unconscious boy out of the room. He lays him on the landing.*

STANLEY. (*Over the body, rapidly and urgently.*) Dear God, let him live. Dear God, let him live . . . please— dear God. I'll never . . .

CLIVE *appears on the landing. He kneels next to his father.*

Oh, God, please!

CLIVE. Walter!

WALTER *stirs.*

STANLEY. He's all right. He's all right.

WALTER. Schon gut. Mir fehlt nichts.

STANLEY. (*Joyfully.*) Boy! . . . Boy. . . .

Woken by the noise, PAMELA *comes from her room into the schoolroom. Sleepily she turns on the light.* CLIVE *moves quickly to prevent her seeing the scene on the landing.*

PAMELA. What is it? What's the matter?

CLIVE. Nothing. It's all right. It's all right. Walter fell down and hurt himself. Just like you did. Now go back to bed. . . . (*Kindly.*) Go on.

She allows herself to be pushed gently back into her bedroom. CLIVE *closes the door.*

CLIVE. (*In a whisper.*) The courage. For all of us. Oh, God—give it.

CURTAIN